A DEFICIT OF DECENCY

Stroud & Hall Publishers
P.O. Box 27210
Macon, GA 31221
www.stroudhall.com

The paper used in this publication meets the minimum requirements
of American National Standard for Information Sciences—
Permanence of Paper for Printed Library Materials.
ANSI Z39.48–1984. (alk. paper)

Library of Congress Cataloging-in-Publication Data

Miller, Zell, 1932-
A deficit of decency / by Zell Miller.
p. cm.
ISBN 0-9745376-3-2 (hardback : alk. paper)
1. Political ethics—United States.
2. United States—Moral conditions.
3. Social values—United States.
I. Title.
JK468.E7M55 2005
172'.0973'090511—dc22

2005003182

Other Books by Zell Miller
The Mountains Within Me (1975), *Great Georgians* (1978),
They Heard Georgia Singing (1980), *Corps Values* (1997)
A National Party No More (2003)

Photo credits: **Savannah Morning News** © Savannah Morning News; **Towns County Herald** © Towns County Herald; **Panoramic Visions** © Panoramic Visions
Photography

A Deficit of Decency

Zell Miller

STROUD&HALL
PUBLISHERS

This book is for my family.

—Zell Miller

Table of Contents

FOREWORD

BY SEAN HANNITY

More than a year before the election of 2004, I said that no senator had had the impact on our country and been a more popular voice among the American people than Zell Miller.

Since then he has had a national best-selling book, made a riveting keynote speech at the Republican National Convention and was one of President Bush's most faithful and effective surrogates in one of history's most important elections.

A Deficit of Decency is the first-person story of this man's extraordinary journey to Washington, D.C., the national spotlight, and back again to his roots in the mountains of North Georgia.

He recounts the inside story of his role in President Bush's re-election campaign and that memorable keynote address—spitballs, duels, and all! He describes in intimate detail what it was like to be caught in the center of a media maelstrom and his eventual redemption as the president's secret weapon in places like rural Ohio and North Florida, where the race for the presidency was decided.

Miller exorcises the debilitating ghosts of Vietnam and pounces on the critics of the war in Iraq; he champions freedom and clearly states the various reasons why freedom has always been a struggle.

He discusses the challenges Democrats will face in 2008, and predicts a methodical metamorphosis of Senator Hillary Rodham Clinton. He takes on gangsta rappers and steroid-popping baseball players. He pointedly argues that the United States should get out of the United Nations and that the IRS should be abolished.

He describes a new and virulent strain of McCarthyism by some in the U.S. Senate that savages judicial nominees who don't agree with their far-left politics. The old Marine sergeant shakes his fist at some of the most difficult and controversial issues of our time—illegal immigration, abortion, radical activist judges, and the well-organized efforts to diminish and destroy Christian values in our society.

At the very core of this marvelous journey is a critique of the soul of our nation, what it will take to build on the freedom and liberty passed on to us by our forefathers and, in turn, leave our children a stronger society. Senator Miller tells us that it all boils down to a test of simple decency and how Washington Doesn't Care (D.C). He says an illness has besieged our nation—a veritable "moral scurvy." But along the way, Senator Miller clearly and convincingly makes the case for the values and issues to live and win by. He discusses his deep faith and how it has become stronger with age and adversity.

In his bestseller, *A National Party No More*, Miller tried to throw a life preserver to a drowning swimmer, but he says that the Democrats didn't even know they were drowning.

His critics will find these plain-spoken words equally as offensive, but sometimes the truth hurts. As the unflinchable senator from Georgia makes his exit from a long and productive career in public office, he leaves us with more than a few things to think, pray, get mad, and even laugh about.

ACKNOWLEDGMENTS

If it is true that we are part of all that we have met—and I believe we are—then there are many I must acknowledge who shaped the thinking that went into this book.

But the thinking would never have become the words on paper and then the print between the covers without my right arm and long-time associate Toni Brown. This dear soul burned the midnight oil and worked more weekends than I can count. Her willingness to do that was crucial, for I write everything in an almost indecipherable long hand and Toni must translate it into English.

There were others. The talented Robert Morris provided encouragement and strong editing skills. Bob Short and Mike Solon added valuable and appreciated advice. Martha Gilland was there as always. And all the folks at Stroud & Hall were patient and helpful.

Shirley's clear-sighted criticism ranged from the caustic to the calming, depending upon what was needed at the time.

But many contributed without even knowing it. Foremost, of course, was that strong, independent woman who raised me and taught me right from wrong. Others include my sister Jane Ross, my Aunt Verdie, and my inspiring and demanding English teacher Edna Herren. There is also Dr. Charles Clegg, the late President of Young

Harris College who gave me my first teaching job and always maintained I'd end up being a preacher, and, of course, the U.S. Marine Corps, whose lessons do last forever. Thanks also to the preachers whose lives are sermons even more inspiring than the ones they preach on Sunday, men like Dow Kirkpatrick, John Kay, Don Harp, and Jimmy Rogers, as well as to the poets, authors, and songwriters whose words have made my heart leap up. My thanks also to the many staff members, who have worked hard over the years to make me look better than I am.

And last, but far from least, my large and loving family—all of them, but especially Murphy, our oldest son, whose passionate pursuit of equal justice makes me proud, and Matthew, our second son, whose quiet and steadfast courage pulls at my heart.

Those whom I have mentioned would probably not agree with everything that I have written in this book, but they know I still love them and I know they love me. Thank God for all His many blessings.

Zell

"WAS BLIND BUT NOW I SEE"

One of my favorite of the great recordings of The Carter Family is "What Would You Give in Exchange for Your Soul?" It gives me chill bumps and causes the hair to rise on the back of my neck. It always has; but in recent years it has become more like a personal short sermon with one of the most penetrating questions that could ever be asked.

This book is about the soul: the soul of our nation, the soul of western civilization, your soul, and my own. In the course of a nation's life, or that of every human being, we are tempted many times and in many ways to exchange or sell our souls, this most precious of all possessions. The payment may be in silver and gold or fame and success.

I believe the bargain is often made with the devil, who comes in various disguises. I believe our souls are inextricably linked to our Maker who created us. I believe it is He who determines where our souls will spend eternity. The soul of a country is different, but I believe God determines its fate as well.

When I was a lad attending revival services at Old Union Baptist Church in Young Harris, Georgia, as the congregation softly sang "Pass Me Not, O Gentle Savior," the preacher or one of the deacons would put his arm around me and ask the most important question one can ever be called to answer—"Are you right with God?"

I often find myself asking that question now, several times a day, not only of myself but of my country. There were two primary reasons I could not go where my lifelong political party wanted to take me. I seriously questioned its judgment on how to respond to the threat of terrorism, the most serious national security issue of the post-Cold War era. But I also came to be repelled by the secularism that had engulfed its thinking and smothered its soul. For me, mocking someone's faith is the most disrespectful thing anyone can do. You can laugh at my accent and ridicule my choice in music, food, or dress, but do not mock my religion. And that was what too many in the Democratic Party, who always proclaimed its great tolerance, did to me and the millions who believe as I do. Disagree, but do not disdain.

So this book, in a most personal way, is about the reawakening of my once dormant spiritual life as well as the realignment of my long-held loyalty to a single political party. It is neither a political treatise nor a religious tract. It's about the journey of one miserable sinner, a flawed pilgrim who took many wrong turns on his way back home.

But this isn't a book about my faith. It's a book about our politics, our country, and our policies. It's a book about my dashed hopes, informed fears, and what I think are solutions. But I can no longer think about these things outside of my faith in God. For too long, politicians have tried to govern while ignoring their faith, teachers have tried to teach while being sworn to camouflage their faith, and parents have tried to raise their children paying more attention to Dr. Phil and Oprah than to the God who blessed them with children. No, I'm not capable of writing an honest book about these things apart from my faith in Jesus Christ. So, as you read, you'll notice references to the Bible and references about my own beliefs and faith. I'm not trying to bolster my arguments with religion. I'm simply sharing with you the only way I know how to look at this great country with which God has blessed and trusted you and me.

My mother saw to it that I was raised to know and do better. As a single parent, she made sure I was a regular at Sharp Memorial United Methodist Church in Young Harris, Georgia—at Sunday School and at church. Later I would be the lay leader of that church and serve on the Board of Stewards. Shirley and I still attend it each and every Sunday, usually with other members of our family.

When I was growing up, my closest friends were all

Zell Bryan Miller, age five.

Baptists, so each Sunday night I would attend Old Union Baptist Church in Young Harris with them. It was a small white wooden building on a rutted dirt road, heated in the winter by a pot-bellied stove and in the summer a cool breeze would come through the open windows. A big bell in the steeple would ring before the "preaching" was to begin. I never missed a summer revival meeting. I still often attend services at this little Baptist church, now a neat brick structure with a paved parking lot, and I can look around the congregation and see five of us who started the first grade together. That's what you call "roots."

I was raised in the churches of the rural South. And I have always loved the old hymns, the lessons of the Bible, and the preachers. They have always touched me deeply. But they did not, I'm sorry to say, touch me deeply enough. I guess I just became one of those "Sunday morning Christians." Enough religion to make me feel comfortable and safe, but not enough to change my ways or make me strictly obey God's words.

As one gets older, as I certainly am—with a lot more years behind me than I have in front of me—it is inevitable that one begins to think more seriously of what life and the hereafter are all about. As the father of two, the grandfather of four, and the great-grandfather of four, not a day goes by that I don't stop to wonder what kind of world we will leave to them. For the last several years, I have seriously contemplated that and it concerns me greatly.

Before the experience the tent maker Saul of Tarsus had on the road to Damascus, he persecuted Christians. He was one of their chief tormentors. We all remember that Saul's life-changing epiphany occurred in a burst of light on that famous road he traveled. My life-changing experience occurred within my family in a burst of blindness—the blindness of my forty-seven-year-old son Matthew, who was first diagnosed with diabetes at the age of five.

Our family knew well how that cruel disease can devastate one's life. Blindness is always a possibility with diabetes, as are kidney failure and poor circulation in the extremities. We knew it, but we were not prepared for it; we thought it would come later, come gradually. We were not prepared in February 2003 when this otherwise healthy man who could read without glasses went completely blind in both eyes within two weeks time. Nothing but darkness. He could not see a thing.

We went to Emory University Hospital in Atlanta with his hands on both my shoulders as I led him around. To make it even worse, his wife would become ill and be in intensive care for seventy-seven days with acute pancreatitis. Several times we thought she was dying.

As we travelled from Emory Hospital with Matt, across town to St. Joseph's Hospital with Katie, our world came crashing in. But in that valley of the shadow of death and blindness, I found there was a rod and staff to comfort me, just as I had always been promised.

Although I've always said my prayers in the morning and evening, often I would say them hurriedly, just sort of thumping them up. But this experience with my family drove me to my knees. Shirley and I prayed and prayed and prayed. And then we prayed some more.

And our prayers were answered. After a long operation and a long recuperative period, I am happy to say sight was restored in one of Matt's eyes. After four operations on the second, we're still not there yet, but we're hopeful. Katie, while still not well, is much better, and they're at home together. Matt is back at work.

Matt was blind and now he sees. And so was I. But today I see things much more clearly than I ever have. I thank God for that and all my many blessings.

I can never forget that God answered our prayers in our greatest time of need. I know there may well be prayers in the future that go unanswered, but my faith in Christ will not be shaken. In 1 Thessalonians 5:17 Paul tells us, "Always be joyful and never stop praying. Whatever happens, keep thanking God because of Jesus Christ. This is what God wants you to do." And I will.

Throughout my life, I have read the Bible sporadically. I'd hear a Scripture text at church or some speaker would use a biblical passage I'd want to check out. I have loved the poetry of David in the Psalms and the Old Testament prophet Amos, especially in the King James Version. But quite frankly, I was not much of a Bible reader. Unlike Shirley, who for years has read it daily, I had no great desire to do so. This has changed also. Now I read it daily, too. Shirley has a systematic reading plan and always a lesson to go with it. I jump from book to book and often go back and read the old familiar passages of which I never tire. But my goal for 2004 was to read the Bible straight through. I read somewhere that one should not say he believes every word of the Bible until he has read every word of the Bible. So much wisdom comes pouring out it's like trying to drink from a fire hydrant. I gulped down "Seek His will in all you do and He will direct your paths" (Proverbs 3:6) and "I know the Lord is always with me. I will not be shaken for He is right beside me" (Proverbs 16:8).

I'm proud to proclaim that, seventy-two years after my birth, I am a Born Again Christian. The old hymn speaks for me when it says, "My hope is built on nothing less than Jesus' blood and righteousness. . . .On Christ the solid Rock, I stand; all other ground is sinking sand." Shirley has long believed and lived that. For years, she waited patiently, often pausing, looking back for me to catch up it seemed.

When it finally happened, I wanted to shout like that great Hank Williams song "I Saw the Light," but I stayed still and quiet to make sure it was not just some temporary emotional thanksgiving for the most important prayer of my life being answered.

It wasn't. And isn't. The "Sunday Morning Christian" I was, is no more. I am now Christian 24/7, strong, almost militant, in my beliefs. That's where the phrase "soldiers of the cross" comes from, I guess. I don't like it when verses like "rise up men of God and put your armor on" and old traditional hymns like "Onward Christian Soldiers" are no longer sung in many of our churches with the feeling and gusto they once were and still deserve. I don't like timidity in anything and that includes religion. Shirley and I believe the Bible is the literal, inerrant word of God, including the book of Revelation. That means we are fundamentalists. Further, we know that we have had and have a personal relationship with Jesus Christ. That makes us evangelicals. We do not hide it; we glory in it. We are proud of it. So when the likes of Ted Turner claim Christianity is "a religion for losers," we'll answer, "Call us what you will."

Among the signers of the Declaration of Independence was a brilliant young physician from Pennsylvania named Benjamin Rush. When Rush was elected to that First Continental Congress, his close friend Benjamin Franklin told him, "We need you. We have a great task before us, assigned to us by Providence." Today, almost 229 years later, I believe there is still a great task before us. I believe it too has been assigned to us by Providence. Our Founding Fathers did not shirk their duty, and we can do no less.

That's why, from its beginning, I was a co-sponsor of the amendment to the Constitution relating to marriage. I was also an original co-sponsor of the Liberties Restoration Act, which declares religious liberty rights in several ways, including the Pledge of Allegiance and the display of the Ten Commandments. And, early in 2004, I worked with Alabama chief justice Roy Moore to come up with the Constitution Restoration Act of 2004 that limits the jurisdiction of federal courts in certain ways, and with then-Senator Richard Shelby who introduced it in the U.S. Senate.

These are the cultural issues of our time. Whether it is removing a display of the Ten Commandments from a courthouse or a nativity scene from a city square, whether it is eliminating prayer in schools or "under God" in the Pledge of Allegiance, whether it is making a mockery of the sacred institution of marriage between a man and woman, or yes, telecasting around the world made-in-the-USA filth masquerading as entertainment, Washington, D.C. doesn't seem to care.

I often chastised the U. S. Senate, once commenting on the floor that "the desire and will of Congress to meaningfully do anything about any of these important issues is nonexistent and embarrassingly disgraceful." I also told them the American people were waiting and growing impatient with us. They wanted something done.

By the way, Benjamin Rush was once asked a question that has long interested me: "Are you a democrat or an aristocrat?" And the good doctor answered, "I am neither. I am a Christocrat. I believe He, alone, who created and redeemed man is qualified to govern him." That reply of Benjamin Rush is just as true today in the year of our Lord 2005 as it was in the year of our Lord 1776.

I have taken a lot of criticism this past year for political expediency, even though I'm not running for anything and consider my political career over. As for some of my old friends and associates, the ties that bind seem to have become unraveled, and I regret that. But this old Marine Sergeant has a tough hide. More importantly, my faith in God is stronger than it has ever been. I take comfort in the words of that great old hymn, "Do thy friends despise, forsake thee. Take it to the Lord in prayer. In His arms He'll take and shield thee. Thou wilt find a solace there."

I have found that "solace," for I am shielded by the grace of God. I am forgiven for my sins. And I am blessed.

Aristotle was once asked to define the difference between a barbaric culture and a civilization. He said that in a barbaric culture, people live from day to day or week to week. They go out and plunder, then they consume what they plundered, and they go out and plunder again. But in a civilization, people go out and they plan and they work for the next generation. They want to pay back what their parents have done for them by doing more for their children. That is how civilization progresses.

There have been ten generations of Americans since this nation was founded, and each one has fulfilled Aristotle's requirement of a civilization. Each left this nation in a little better condition than when they inherited it from their parents. This is the first generation at risk of doing the opposite. Why? I have come to believe the reason is we have failed to acknowledge and discipline ourselves with the spiritual truths that made us great for these two hundred years— faith, family, country, values. This book is about how one man thinks they may be restored and how we may yet save this great civilization—from itself.

Zell Miller, U.S. Senator
January 2005

A DEFICIT OF DECENCY

When bad men combine, the good must associate; else they will fall one by one, an unpitied sacrifice in a contemptible struggle.

— Edmund Burke (1729–1797)

Edmund Burke was right. When the bad combine, the good must associate. This book is a sounding alarm to the good. Just like you, I've watched this great nation of ours begin to rot from the inside out. While technology continues to revolutionize and improve our quality of life, the more important and eternal values of character and decency are becoming things of the past. Like flood waters, the tell-tale signs of a deficit of decency seem to arise from everywhere. These chapters are my attempt to describe the "big issues"— how duty as a character is dying, how Washington Doesn't Care, and how the Christian values on which this country was founded are being ignored. In these chapters, I expose the places where the deficit grows. In these places, I pray the good may once again stand fast and tall.

Chapter 1

THE DEATH OF DUTY

A story in the Bible says so well what I want to say about duty. Jesus and his disciples receive word from Mary and Martha that their brother Lazarus has died. On hearing this, Jesus knows at once what he must do: go to where Lazarus is and resurrect him. He tells his disciples this.

One would expect all the disciples would be eager to go. But they are not. Instead, they are gloomy and obviously frightened. This magnetic leader to whom they've been drawn has become dangerous. For them, it would mean going back through those Judean hills and once again facing the hostility and the threat of being stoned or even executed.

I think that's why we love these disciples. They are so much like us, so very human. Immediately, excuses not to go were forthcoming. One said, "Maybe he's just sick and will get better. That happens to a lot of people." Some nodded their heads in agreement, eager to persuade Jesus to change his mind.

There was one disciple, however, who stood with Jesus. That one has come to be remembered mostly as "Doubting Thomas." I have always thought that was an unfair nickname. Thomas, while not mentioned as much as some of the other disciples, is in some key stories in the Bible. Several times he displayed a practical and inquisitive personality. Remember, he is the one who interrupted Jesus, "Lord, we do not know where you are going; how can we know the way?" This question gave Jesus the chance to answer with one of the most important statements in the entire Bible—"I am the way, the truth, and the life. . . ."

So when Jesus announced he was heading back to Bethany to see about Lazarus, this lone "disciple of duty," as I call him, said, "Let us also go that we may die with him."

The other disciples must not have been able to believe their ears. What's with Thomas, they must have thought. Didn't he understand the danger? Had he forgotten all the threats? Did he have some kind of false hope?

He had none of the above. What Thomas had was a sense of duty. When hope fades, duty stands fast. Thomas said, "Let us also go," because, quite simply, it was the right thing to do. Thomas did it because he was decent and had a sense of duty. He didn't require credit or compensation for doing what he knew was right. Thomas, that loyal but practical man, knew it then, and you and I know it now. Sometimes duty is enough.

Duty *is* enough. This simple notion is all but lost in America today. It has not always been so. This famous quotation from Nathan Hale once was taught to every school child: "I regret that I have but one life to give for my country." I learned this quote in the fifth grade. It was an inspiration to me then; it's an inspiration to me today. I think other young people might carry it around with them for life, just as I have, if this important quotation were still taught today. No danger of that. Today, such a conviction would be considered corny.

One place it is not considered corny is at West Point, where since 1898 the legend in the code of arms has read "Duty, Honor, Country." The great columnist William Safire has called that "the trinity of patriotism."

The brave words of Thomas remind me of what our good Lord had in mind from the beginning. That law-giving Old Testament book of Deuteronomy well describes what we are about as Americans because it includes guidelines on how to live, raise children, and take care of the place.

> You shall love the Lord your God with all your heart and with all your soul and with all your might. These words which I am commanding you today, shall be on your heart. You shall teach them diligently to your sons and shall talk of them when you sit in your house and when you walk by the way and when you lie down and when you rise up. You shall bind them as a sign on your hand and they shall be as frontals on your forehead. You shall write them in the doorways of your house and on your gates.

Basically, the Lord is telling his children to make His ways our way of life, not something we just think or believe, but something we do and do naturally. When we lie down and when we rise up, we should be surrounded by it.

For me, that's inclusive enough to include Washington, D.C. When the Lord tells his children to make their faith a way of life, not something they just think about or give lip service to, but something they do and do naturally, it should include the capital city of our country and what goes on in its hallowed halls. But it doesn't seem to.

Duty and decency came naturally to those who founded America. Our American dream is possible because someone who didn't know us and whose name we will never know shed blood, sweat, and tears so that we can warm our hands in fires we didn't build and drink from wells we did not dig.

And then, of course, there are those whose names we once knew and revered but today are all but forgotten. Their thoughts and theories discarded into that over-flowing dustbin of history. Today it's all about "political" correctness, not just correctness. We're walking in their tracks, but we can't fill their shoes. And, regrettably, we don't even want to. Madison, Hamilton, Adams, Washington. They're yesterday.

I have always felt that duty was like an anvil dangling over my head, held by a sewing thread. Whenever I see duty being ignored, it troubles me. It worries me. It frustrates me. And today I see it all around me. I see it in shopping malls, on the Capital Beltway, and on the athletic fields and courts occupied by self-centered millionaires who cheat with corked bats and steroid enhanced bodies.

A preacher once told me of a single dad to whom he had been ministering. The young dad had the custodial rights he needed and ample opportunities to spend frequent weekends with his school-aged son. But he seldom did so. One day the preacher asked him, "Why don't you ever have your son over and do something special with him? Don't you think he would like it?" The dad looked at him and answered, "Well, I guess I could do that, but I'd just be doing it out of a sense of duty."

Have you ever heard anything sadder? Shrugging off responsibility in such an off-handed way. But this lack of a sense of personal duty is growing more and more common. What would be wrong with that father doing something simply out of "a sense of duty"?

I can understand that perhaps there could be higher levels of motivation. Maybe the opportunity to coach the child in Little League or take him camping or spend more than just every other weekend with him? But if these higher things aren't possible, what's wrong with doing something lesser out of a sense of duty? What's wrong with doing something *simply because it ought to be done*?

There was a time and a place where a sense of duty was enough. That time was not long ago, and the place was America. Countless numbers of folks have done the boring, the uninviting, the unenlightening, and the unrecognized thing to make America what it is.

We wouldn't be who we are today without them. And we'll stop being who we are if more of us don't start picking up our share.

So here I come with a book about decency and duty in a world that has been weaned on convenience and selfishness. There was a time when I thought I was pretty much alone with these thoughts. Shirley, my lighthouse on a stormy coast, believed it and had for years. As usual, I was the slow learner. But then finally I saw it, clear as day. Did you ever have that feeling, like you were the only one in the world who felt a certain way about a thing? It reminds me of that wise quip, "If everyone's against you, paranoia is simply good thinking."

Well, in February 2004, I got fed up. I had had enough. The Apostle Paul called it an "utter groaning" and wrote in Romans that sometimes the Spirit churns something in us that must come out even if mere words can't capture it adequately. That is exactly what happened to me. It was a time when I knew I had to speak regardless of how it struck my colleagues in the Senate, how unsophisticated it might sound to them, or how it might affect me personally or politically. My faith, my duty, and my respect for decency demanded that I speak. So I stood on the floor of the United States Senate in February 2004 and delivered a speech that became the guiding vision for this book. I called it "A Deficit of Decency." Here are the beginning and closing comments of that speech:

> The Old Testament prophet Amos was a sheep herder who lived back in the Judean hills, away from the larger cities of Bethlehem and Jerusalem. Compared to the intellectual urbanites like Isaiah and Jeremiah, he was just an unsophisticated country hick.
>
> But Amos had a unique grasp of political and social issues, and his poetic literacy skill was among the best of all the prophets. That familiar quote of Martin Luther

King Jr. about "Justice will rush down like waters and righteousness like a mighty stream" are Amos's words.

Amos was the first to propose the concept of a universal God and not just some tribal deity. He also wrote that God demanded moral purity, not rituals and sacrifices. This blunt-speaking moral conscience of his time warns in chapter 8, verse 11 of the book of Amos, as if he were speaking to us today, that "the days will come, sayeth the Lord God, that I will send a famine in the land. Not a famine of bread, nor a thirst for water, but of hearing the word of the Lord. And they shall wander from sea to sea, and from the north even to the east. They shall run to and fro to seek the word of the Lord, and shall not find it."

"A famine in the land." Has anyone more accurately described the situation we face in America today? "A famine of hearing the words of the Lord."

But some will say Amos was just an Old Testament prophet—a minor one at that—who lived seven hundred years before Christ. That is true, so how about one of the most influential historians of modern times?

Arnold Toynbee, who wrote the acclaimed twelve-volume *A Study of History*, once declared, "Of the twenty-two civilizations that have appeared in history, nineteen of them collapsed when they reached the moral state America is in today."

Toynbee died in 1975, before seeing the worst that was yet to come. Yes, Arnold Toynbee saw the famine. The "famine of hearing the words of the Lord."

So, if I am asked why—with all the pressing problems this nation faces today—why am I pushing these social issues and taking the Senate's valuable time? I will answer: Because it is of the highest importance. Yes, there's a deficit to be concerned about in this country, a deficit of decency.

So, as the sand empties through my hourglass at warp speed—and with my time running out in this Senate and on this earth—I feel compelled to speak out. For I truly believe that at times like this, silence is not golden. It is yellow.

Never in my wildest imagination could I have predicted the outcome of that speech. I hadn't thought about it much because, quite frankly, that is not why I gave it. But it quickly became evident that I was not the only one thinking about these things in this way. I was not the only one who had recognized the signs that decency and duty in our country are on their deathbeds. I was not the only one who knew that our children, grandchildren, and great-grandchildren face certain danger, hardship, and struggle if a sense of decency and responsibility isn't restored across our land. I was not the only one, as it turned out, with an "utter groaning."

How did I know this? In the few days after delivering this speech, I received 16,000 emails of support, affirmation, and thanksgiving. Countless folks around the country copied and forwarded the text of the speech to others over the Internet. Dr. D. James Kennedy, that respected man of God, ran it on his network of more than seven hundred radio stations. There's no way to know how far-reaching my simple comments really were. Like one of those forest fires out West that won't stop burning, that speech roared on and on.

I soon came to realize it needed to be expanded, researched, and applied. Many others had already done it better than ever I could, but perhaps I had a forum they had not had. Where are we now as a country? How did we get here? There are important questions to ask ourselves. My elected term is over, and I'm now back in the mountains of the great state of Georgia where I came from. This book, among other things, is about what I see as a growing deficit of decency in our country, its consequences, and what we can do to change it.

Chapter 2

WASHINGTON DOESN'T CARE

Some things should never change about how Washington goes about its work. Inside the beltway should always be a respected place for honest representation and lawmaking on behalf of the people. It should be a place where doing the right thing with a sense of duty is first and foremost. *Should be.*

I learned a long time ago that no matter where you go or what you do, as long as there is someone to serve, there will be somebody complaining. This is an ageless problem. Jesus faced it, too. In Matthew 12, a painfully afflicted person was brought to Jesus for healing. Jesus restored his sight and speech. The crowds were amazed. Hardly room to register a complaint, right? Wrong! Even a miracle performed by Jesus drew the whiners—the Pharisees "across the aisle" who started grumbling. If the Pharisees had lived in Washington, D.C., they might have said, "Wait a minute! We were going to get this man a seeing eye dog. Do you want to put the folks who train those dogs out of business? They've got a union and they've got a political action committee. They give us money and help get out the vote."

But Jesus answered the whiners with a lesson on what happens when a house forgets its foundation and becomes divided against itself. He knew what they were thinking and said to them, "Every kingdom divided against itself is laid waste, and no city or house divided against itself will stand. . . . Whoever is not with me is against me, and whoever does not gather with me scatters . . . ."

There is so much America needs right now, and yet so little is getting done. So much time is wasted. So much money is wasted. Just as a fish rots from the head down, the head of our government (Washington, D.C.) is decaying. John Randolph of Roanoke once described his archenemy, Henry Clay, as one who "shines and stinks like a dead mackerel in the moonlight." That's an apt description of Washington, D.C. at the beginning of the twenty-first century. Those ornate halls and marble floors may shine, but I am sorry to say they are also beginning to smell.

After four years of monitoring D.C.'s heartbeat, I can tell you decency is dying from the inside out, and Washington doesn't care. Sometimes I think that's what the D.C. stands for—*Doesn't Care.* Congress keeps fiddling with the trim and changing the paint while the foundation of good and honest service burns. We didn't get this way overnight, and we won't fix it overnight either. But we can fix it, and we must.

How did we get in this mess? Seemingly by every road possible. Take, for example, the initiation of a newly-elected United States senator. At long last, you've made it to the Capitol with the best of intentions, ready to change the world. You've worked hard to earn the trust and respect of your state's voters, and now you're ready to get about the business of doing good for your folks back home.

But in the first five minutes of your arrival, while meeting your party's leaders, you are shocked to learn that the campaign you just worked your heart out to win is really not over. Your first and most important job, you are told, is to get, of all things, reelected. And not just yourself, but all the others on "the team," whether you are on their side of an issue or not. If they wear the team colors, you are not only expected to help them, you are *obligated* to help them. You are told that the main goal is to remain politically viable and keep the issues alive so you and *all* your party members can first and foremost assure reelection. Doing the work of the people back home is never mentioned. Wearing the "team" colors and becoming "reelectable" is not only your first but your *only* goal. This goal, you are told, is complicated and very expensive.

Have you paid much attention to what some folks do these days to get elected? Getting elected today isn't like it was fifty years ago, or even five years ago. Like everything, our changing culture has made itself known. Take, for example, how our telecommunications industry has skyrocketed. Pagers, the Internet, satellite television, cable, twenty-four-hour news networks—all of these have done their number on today's political process.

I'm reminded of a man I know back home named Mac whose wife worked at the hospital at the county seat. Like many hospital employees, she carried a pager at work. A pager is designed to enable some other person to perform what I call "strategic interruption." I personally refuse to carry the "intruder" around with me. It is not welcome. But for Mac's wife, the intruder was considered a necessary evil. So one afternoon, Mac paged his wife at work. But something went technologically AWOL, and Mac's phone number went to every hospital employee who had a pager. Suddenly, Mac's phone was fat with calls from every kind of medical professional imaginable, all calling him from within the same building. He talked to the X-ray tech, accounts receivable, anesthesiology, a pediatric nurse, and someone who apparently worked on the hospital's building and ground department. By the time this was over, Mac, like me, didn't care for pagers very much. For thirty minutes his phone rang every few seconds, but none of those calls were from his wife. Mac, like too many of Washington's congressional leaders, talked to everyone except to those who really mattered.

So if Washington doesn't care about the people back home, what does it care about? Reelection? Certainly. Special interests? Yes, that is, if they have a sizeable bank account. To be supported and slobbered over by every group they come in contact with?

Absolutely! Isn't that, after all, what it's all about—to be loved by all? What else could explain Michael Dukakis's willingness to look like a bobble head in a tank? Why would Bill Clinton freely discuss his preferences in undershorts in a television studio filled with young adults? And why, pray tell, did John Kerry show up looking like a Saturday Night Live skit gone bad, a Hells Angel caricature, a bandito nomad donning a leather jacket, lace-up boots, and propped up on top of a Harley Hog? The problem is that today there are simply more groups to get in front of and try to be loved by than ever before.

There's now a satellite channel, a radio station, a website or a blog for every niche group imaginable. Once upon a time—long, long ago, it now seems—the news and nothing but the news, for the most part, came to us via three networks. Then came the enterprising Ted Turner with a twenty-four-hour cable headquarters, in of all places Scarlett O'Hara's Atlanta, Georgia. Then came a channel for every message imaginable. From Jesus to jewelry, from home improvement to home wrecking, from self-help to self-destruction, from hip hop to hard rock, from holistic healing to alien hostage taking, from stupid pet tricks to stupid legal tricks—you name it, and you'll find a politician willing to appear on it.

Now, cable's not a bad thing. In fact, I've come to like it and depend on it. But, like most anything else, it can be used for good or for bad. A particularly troubling trend today is something I call CCC, or, *Constant Cable Confusion.* CCC is basically the propensity for stations and networks to blur the lines between news and entertainment to where it is practically impossible to determine fact from fiction.

MTV started inserting news between videos years ago. Now, I'm not picking on MTV (not here, but don't run off, their time's coming). I'm simply crying out that not only does the "emperor have no clothes," but an entire generation of young adults have gotten the news of their world from a visual juke box.

Techies have got Tech TV; sports fans have ESPN; home improvement fanatics have HGTV; and history nuts like me have the History Channel. News junkies can surf multiple places for twenty-four-hour news. Programming, perspective, or the lack thereof, is even tailored to meet particular tastes.

"No spin zone" and "fair and balanced" have become a part of our national vocabulary, and I think they should be. But who could have said with a straight face twenty years ago, "I think I'll start a show on a network that does nothing but comedy, and we'll cover real news events, but do it for an audience that prefers fake news." Here's Jon Stewart hitting it out of the park every night—and now also in a bestselling mock "textbook"— because Washington keeps tossing him the slow pitch. It's a shame we make his work that easy.

Again, there's nothing inherently wrong with 220 channels beaming into your home every day and night. But don't think for a minute that it is not having an effect on our culture and warping the way we view the world. Go ahead and eat my lunch, socio-psycho-babbleologists, but CCC is rubbing some kind of strange groove into our collective mind and imagination. Allow me to explain. Did you ever mistakenly surf to a channel on your cable dial that is dedicated to stuff in which you have absolutely no interest? Did you find it hard to follow? Did you wonder what they were talking about? It's not limited to television. I once heard part of a sports talk radio program whose format was dedicated to listeners calling in and ranting about sports in something between poetic verse and locker room bullery. What I heard in no way helped me understand how to hit a ball better or who won the game. It was a sports show that had little to do with sports. I didn't understand it.

If you're not a computer whiz, and I fit that description, turn to Tech TV and watch for five minutes. You'll have to get your grand-children or your neighbor's kids to interpret. CCC has spawned a series of new and indiscernible languages that is rendering us less capable of talking to one another because we're accustomed to hearing and learning things in ways that are tailored just to us.

So back to my main thesis. If you're a politician trying to get elected and look appealing to these many audiences, you are required to reinvent yourself two, three, or more times a day in order to appeal to whatever audience you're in front of at the time. Learning the language of every new interest group is part of the job description for elected officials in Washington, D.C. Babble on, oh Babylon—we're praying to a Tower of Babble!

Like my farmer friend, Mac, we're talking to everyone and no one. We end up with political candidates who are mosaics of numerous sound bites rather than portraits of centered and steadied public servants. As the Ragin' Cajun James Carville diagnosed the Harley-riding Hells Angel wannabe shortly after the election, John Kerry relied on a litany rather than a narrative to tell his story.

Playing to CCC, or Constant Communication Confusion, has become a self-fulfilling prophecy. The more politicians appear on these niche programs, the more they appeal to the extremes of their base who are in turn motivated to raise enough money to fund enough ads to get in front of all these different audiences. Thus, these office holders/seekers end up motivating the base of extremes and in effect alienate themselves from the middle where most of the people are. The harder they try to reach the middle, where there are no organized special interests or PACs, the more it costs. When the election is over the cycle starts all over again, like the hamster forever spinning on that little wheel.

During your initiation to the Washington that doesn't care, you are instructed to ask for more and more money from special interest groups. Every political consultant working in Washington today tells their client within the first ten minutes of their first meeting, "Raise money and get on TV; that's what it's all about." Forget everything else. Nothing else matters. More money means a better chance of surviving the next election cycle. But the end result is that these dollars sprout roots—deep roots—and keep you from swaying or drifting too far from the narrow goals of the special interest groups who give the money. And God help you if you do. They will descend upon you with the wrath of a spitting cobra.

We end up with a governing body paralyzed by political correctness as defined by these groups, rather than the people back home. In effect, our elected leaders lease out their influence over the lawmaking process, hoping to get enough money to reach enough slices of our country to come back and do the same thing all over again. And we wonder why voters care less and less every year.

Chapter 3

IS IT DECENT?

Paul wrote two-thirds of the New Testament. The footprint he made on the Christian faith is unparalleled. Where would we be without him? His letters to the churches of the first century are full of ageless wisdom about what it means to be a Christian and how to go about your faith. Of all the great words he wrote, none stand taller than the simple phrase "Let us behave decently."

Did you ever notice that when the subject matter is eternal truth, there's no time for beating around the bush? When what you're saying is the stuff of truth that stands the test of time, it doesn't take many words to say it. Some people say Christianity is complicated. Jesus said it can be summed up simply, "Love thy neighbor as thyself."

When it comes to eternal and important things, a few words will do. If you don't believe me, just notice how many words people use when they're running *from* the truth. When someone is trying to pass something off as truth that they know good and well is a sack of lies, watch how carefully and how *much* they speak. When someone is lying, words are used to cover up the truth. Words are twisted and sliced through. When someone is lying, things like precision suddenly become important. Precision allows liars to keep the trial going a little longer. Truth isn't careful or precise. It doesn't have to be. Who can forget the thoughtful and careful words "That depends on what the meaning of 'is' is"? I rest my case.

Paul didn't have to be careful when he wrote, "Let us behave decently." In those few words, he left nowhere to hide, no wiggle room. With those few words Paul gave us a moral compass for navigating our homes, our communities, and our world. What could possibly be added to "Let us behave decently" that matters? What could possibly be added to those words that would make them cut more deeply? What could possibly be added to make the foundation any firmer? Only those running from truth would find comfort and strength in their own wordiness.

The reason I am writing this book is that I believe America has been struck by a profound and debilitating lack of decency, and it's making us weak. I'm not talking about or worried about a few isolated acts of indecency. In our brightest moments as a nation, there were isolated moments of indecency. What I'm talking about today is a prolonged, sustained, and seemingly unending age in which a lack of decency has become the norm. It's like the difference between a dry spell and a drought. One is noticed. The other is devastating.

High hopes have been deflated by low standards, and the result is a nation starving for decency. America has a bad case of moral scurvy, and nobody seems to have a cure. In this book, I will point to the places where decency and duty are gasping for air like a couch potato in a marathon. This lack of decency is morphing from a random occurrence to a way of life, a brand new national pastime.

Pretty soon this moral scurvy simply becomes an acceptable condition. Nobody notices. It becomes the water in which we swim. Do you think a fish knows he's wet? Of course not. As a country, we're drowning and we don't even know it. We're numb and we can't even feel it. We're driving down the highway to hell and haven't noticed or don't care that "the bridge to the future" is out. In this book, I'm simply trying to prop up the "bridge out" sign.

There is one place where a lack of decency can transform failure into absolute failure, a failure so thorough that time doesn't seem to budge. A failure to handle our United States Constitution with decency will create for us a kind of deficit that no amount of gross national product will solve. Our Constitution is the stuff of eternal truth. The framers of the Constitution knew something of the truth. They knew that America was called to be the shining example to the world of governments and societies. They knew that America could be a secure place for liberty to be nurtured, tended, and experienced. They knew that when freedom and responsibility were fused, the blessing would be liberty above all else. They knew God created in each of us the hunger for freedom. With the right mix of personal responsibility and decency, this experiment that many deemed foolish could work, even thrive. It did. It has. The question is, will it continue?

The framers knew precisely the principles upon which to base that important document. But they didn't and couldn't know precisely all of the ways it would be applied. There was no way for them to be able to predict America's future. They couldn't have. They didn't need to. Principles are not situational. They aren't swayed by shifting sands of taste, preference, license, or newly spawned notions of entitlement. The framers of the Constitution couldn't have predicted all the odd and ignoble manners in which the Constitution would be applied. They couldn't have known how the world would shift, how America would change, or the crossroads we would face. Sometimes it feels to me like we're marching off the map. The legendary Ray Charles put it this way, "Look what they've done to my song, ma. The only thing I could do half right and now it's turning out all wrong, mama. Look what they've done to my song."

What do we do when we come to the edge of the Constitution? What do we do when we face a crossroads for which there is no specific language for guidance? We make laws. Folks like me are charged with the responsibility of knowing what the folks back

home think, what they want, what they'll support. Elected representatives are sent to the Capitol to make laws for us all to live by that
are based on the more timeless and eternal principles laid out in the
Constitution.

Simple enough, right? Not so. Those timeless truths devolve into
tit for tat. Principles vanish, and the eternal evaporates into an orgy
of special interests. Lawmakers find themselves wading through the
shallow, murky waters. In Washington, D.C., there is a sort of seduc-
tive atmosphere, and you can forget where you came from, who you
represent, and what you really wanted to accomplish.

Also, the mood of this growing and increasingly diverse country
has a way of shifting. To give lawmakers credit, the mood of the
country is a moving target, and representing a moving target can be
tough. Laws can get crafted that satisfy a national sentiment only
later to seem out of step with common experience and even
common sense. No matter what the reasons are, imperfect leaders
for an imperfect country often craft imperfect laws.

When the oddball legislation comes through the Capitol and
misses the target or misses the will of the people or pinches some
special interest group, it gets challenged. The U.S. Supreme Court is
where federal law is supposed to be interpreted and held up to the
light that shines from the Constitution to see if it is the stuff of
truth. When it comes to whether a law fits or not, the popular question has become, *Is it constitutional?*

It's a good question. But it's the wrong question. It's the wrong
question because those who look for X in the Constitution usually
end up finding it. Activist judges tend to "discover" whatever they
want to find, and unfortunately, that something is usually themselves. It's like a group picture. When you look at a group picture in
which you appear, what's the first thing you look for? Me, too. So
when the envious activist asks, "Is it really constitutional?" he or she
is really asking, "Constitution, Constitution on the wall, isn't my
interpretation the fairest of them all?" Those explorers of the question set out with an idea of what the outcomes are before making

the trip. Too often, the question leads to a kind of justification that stretches the limits of common sense or human decency.

Ideas come through our courts that are as far from the Constitution as Young Harris, Georgia, is from Washington, D.C. You can always tell when a law is somewhere outside the light of the framers. It reads like it's been stretched and crammed and beat into something it's not. The stuff of truth is simple and takes few words. Asking "Is it constitutional?" is sometimes the wrong question because smart folks can make convincing arguments for contradictory ideas. It becomes like a church fight with both sides quoting Scripture.

So what's the answer? Or better yet, what's the right question? The right question for addressing the Constitution is one that is burdened with responsibility. The right question when addressing a new law or idea about our great country is one that cuts through the distraction of the details of language and nuance and gets straight to the timeless principles. The "light of the Constitution," I call it. The right question for addressing the Constitution is simple and natural and greets with joy those principles endowed to us by our Creator and intended by our Founding Fathers.

Is it decent? is the right question. It's one that all of us know and can answer, law degree or not. It's a question that removes the hiding places created by the hedges of legal language. It's a question that doesn't require long or ornate responses. *Is it decent?* is a question that bridges our future with our past. It asks, "Is this the kind of thing that got us here? Is this the kind of thing that will get us to where we want to be?" *Is it decent?* keeps us in touch with the sense of rightness for which God created us.

Is it decent? demands not wordy responses or over-educated legal beagles to interpret it, but simple truth, which doesn't need many words and doesn't lean into the technical. It doesn't argue about the meaning of "is." Paul said, "Let us behave decently." There's a deficit of that right now in this nation and in Washington, Doesn't Care.

THE HIGH CALLING OF DECENCY: SUPPORTING PRESIDENT BUSH

For everything, there is a season, a time
for every matter under heaven.

— Ecclesiastes 3:1

I did something in 2004 that I've always been willing to do if I thought it was the right thing, but never had to do. I guess there really is a time for everything. Last November, it was time for this lifelong Democrat not only to vote for a Republican candidate, but to campaign for him as well. Doing the right thing means being willing to sacrifice, even when inconvenient. Sometimes a sense of duty calls us forward. What politician in the twilight of his career wants to step out on an unpopular limb? Basic decency and love for America have called me to risk friendships and a lifetime as a party leader to do what I knew was right. These chapters are a diary of sorts that include my experience and my thoughts concerning this most recent presidential election and future elections as well.

Chapter 4:

A DISCERNING DEMOCRAT
DECIDES

I have been a Democrat since the day I was born, February 24, 1932. But by the fall of 2003, it became painfully obvious to me that my lifelong allegiance was being cannibalized, eaten alive by the special interests and their own narrow agenda. The more I listened to the liberal claptrap at the Tuesday luncheon caucuses and how and why they cast their votes, the more uncomfortable I became with the national party.

So I broke with the leaders of my party on tax cuts, workplace ergonomics rules, the environment, and the president's appointees. But the straw that broke the camel's back was the caucus on homeland security. What came to be the main point of contention was whether any of the 170,000-plus employees of the new Department of Homeland Security could be moved around by the president in a time of national emergency, whether all the hide-bound restrictions of an obsolete Civil Service System would complicate and delay our national security. Every president before George W. Bush had that kind of authority, but because 2002 was an election year, the employee's labor union wanted to flex its muscles. They wanted to have a fight because that helps increase their membership. The Daschle Democrats could smell that soft money, and for eleven votes over a period of nearly four months they delayed this critical piece of legislation. During that time, I was the one and only Democrat who voted with the president and against my own party.

The midterm elections came and went and two Democratic senators, Max Cleland of Georgia and Jean Carnihan of Missouri, were defeated largely because of this vote. Immediately after the election, the bill passed without the Democrats saying the first word about protection for union employees. Just weeks before, they had treated it as a life-or-death issue, important enough, in their minds, to subvert efforts to improve homeland security. It had all been simply politics, bought and paid for by liberal special interests. Then and there I decided I would never attend another Democratic caucus lunch. I had seen and heard enough.

Shortly thereafter, the period of sickness I wrote about earlier hit my immediate family. Our son Matt and his wife Katie were both hospitalized for an extended period of several months. Shirley and I spent a lot of time in the intensive care waiting room at Emory University and St. Joseph's hospitals in Atlanta.

As we waited, hopeful that our prayers would be answered, I began to write down what I had seen, heard, and learned during my first two years in Washington. Having spent my life working on behalf of Democrats and the Democratic Party, I naturally assumed it was my duty to explain to myself and others what had happened. Eventually, it became a book. At first, I called it *The Conscience of a Conservative Democrat*; later I added *A National Party No More* as its main title because I sincerely believed my party had abandoned me and many others who shared my view of what the party should be. I had hoped it would be a wakeup call, a message of how to take our party back, how to make it strong and competitive again. I wanted to throw a life preserver to a drowning swimmer about to go under for the third and last time.

But the swimmer wouldn't reach for the preserver. In fact, he didn't even know he was drowning. After that book was published, I was told in no uncertain terms, "Take that life-preserver and stick it where the sun doesn't shine."

In late October 2003, I was invited to be on *Hannity & Colmes* on the Fox News Channel. Sean Hannity came to my Washington office for an interview about the book. It proceeded routinely until he asked the question, "Who will you support for president next year?" I spontaneously replied, "President Bush." And the roof caved in.

After blurting out to Sean what I had been considering since 9/11 and the experience with my Democratic colleagues over the homeland security bill, I realized that I should put in writing an explanation for my decision. So in an op-ed piece for the *Wall Street Journal*, I began, "If I live and breathe, and if—as Hank Williams used to say—the creek don't rise, in 2004 this Democrat will do something I didn't do in 2000; I will vote for George W. Bush for president."

I continued,

> I have come to believe that George Bush is the right man in the right place at the right time. And that's a pretty big mouthful coming from a lifelong Democrat who first voted for Adlai Stevenson in 1952 and has voted for every Democratic presidential candidate the twelve cycles since then. My political history to the contrary, this was the easiest decision I think I've ever made in deciding who to support. For I believe that the next five years will determine the kind of world my four grandchildren and four great-grandchildren will live in. I simply cannot entrust that crucial decision to any one of the current group of Democratic presidential candidates.

"I keep trying to tell you...that's not how it's done down South!"

And then I added a personal note,

> I first got to know George Bush when we served as governors together, and I just plain like the man, a man who feeds his dogs first thing every morning, has Larry Gatlin sing in the White House, and knows what is meant by the term "hitting behind the runner."

I then turned to the political,

> This is a president who understands the price of freedom. He understands that leaders throughout history often have had to choose between good and evil, tyranny and freedom. And the choice they make can reverberate for generations to come. This is a president who has some Churchill in him and who does not flinch when the going

gets tough. This is a president who can make a decision and does not suffer from "analysis paralysis." This is a president who can look America in the eye and say on Iraq, "We're not leaving." And you know he means it.

I continued,

This is also a president who understands that tax cuts are not just something that all taxpayers deserve, but also the best way to curb government spending. It is the best kind of tax reform. If the money never reaches the table, Congress can't gobble it up.

But why not vote for one of my fellow Democrats? I tried to explain,

Believe me, I looked hard at the other choices. And what I saw was that the Democratic candidates who want to be president in the worst way are running for office in the worst way. Look closely, there's not much difference among them. I can't say there's "not a dime's worth of difference" because there's actually billions of dollars' worth of difference among them. Some want to raise our taxes a trillion, while the others want to raise our taxes by several hundred billion. But make no mistake; they all want to raise our taxes. They also, to varying degrees, want us to quit and get out of Iraq. They don't want us to stay the course in this fight between tyranny and freedom. This is our best chance to change the course of history in the Middle East. So I cannot vote for a candidate who wants us to cut and run with our shirttails at half-mast.

Then I predicted what would happen exactly one year later—and why none of the Democratic candidates was acceptable.

I find it hard to believe, but these naïve nine have managed to combine the worst feature of the McGovern campaign—the president is a liar and we must have peace at any cost—with the worst feature of the Mondale campaign—watch your wallet, we're going to raise your taxes. George McGovern carried one state in 1972. Walter Mondale carried one state in 1984. Not exactly role models when it comes to how to get elected or, for that matter, how to run a country. So, as I have said, my choice for president was an easy decision. And my own party's candidates made it even easier.

Now, I have never been one simply to endorse a candidate and then sit on my hands and not try to help my candidate win. My book *A National Party No More* was reaching more people than I had ever dreamed it would. Somehow it had struck a chord with many who recognized that our party had taken a sharp turn left, leaving a good many of us behind. The book quickly went to number four on the *New York Times* nonfiction best-seller list and remained on the list for nine weeks.

Many Democrats—most who had not even read it—wanted to kill the messenger without ever reading the message. But for every negative comment, there were a dozen positive ones, not only in Georgia but, surprising to me, throughout the nation. They came from Republicans, Independents, and Democrats alike. Although I've had a long and controversial lifetime in politics, I had never seen anything like it. To the national Democratic Party, I was an instant outcast, persona non-gratis, public enemy number one.

In January 2004, an old friend, former Montana governor Marc Racicot, the chairman of the Bush Cheney campaign, called and asked if I would meet with him and Ken Mehlman, the campaign manager. I did not know Ken Mehlman, but I knew of his excellent reputation as a meticulous, detailed professional operative. We were to meet at the Republican National Committee Headquarters on

First Street. I thought I knew the location, but since this Democrat had never been to the RNC Headquarters before, I ended up going into the wrong building. "Can you tell me how to get to the National Republican Headquarters?" I asked the security guard. I must admit, never in my wildest dreams could I have imagined asking such a question. But I quickly recovered from my slightly perplexed state and was directed next door to the right place.

Racicot and Mehlman thanked me again and wanted to find out how much I was willing to do in the campaign. I quickly told them my highest priority was to see this president reelected and I would do "whatever you think will help." Marc quickly responded by asking if I would head up the Democrats for Bush. "If you think it'll help," I replied.

"Would you be a speaker at our national convention?" Mehlman followed up. I quickly answered, "They"—meaning the Democrats and media—"will run my '92 speech over and over." Racicot and Mehlman had already considered that possibility. "But would you do it?" Mehlman asked again and I repeated, "I said I would do anything you think will help." I would come back to that statement over and over again during the most volatile election year any one of us had ever seen. Obviously, they thought it would help, and we left it at that and moved into planning the Democrats for Bush announcement.

On March 4, 2004, at the Park Hyatt Hotel only a few blocks from the Capitol, I laid out to a group of Democrats and members of the media why this longtime partisan Democrat was supporting a Republican president's reelection. Governor Racicot made the announcement and introduced me. Then I talked about how Marc and I had been governors and how each of us understood the importance of strong executive leadership.

I told the gathering that I was honored to stand squarely with President George W. Bush as he leads America "at this defining moment in our history." I talked about how the road that had brought me there had been paved "with a lot of frustration, but also a lot of hope."

I said, and would say hundreds of times in the course of the campaign, "I was born a Democrat, and I expect I'll be a Democrat until the day I leave this earth." But I told them I had grown mighty frustrated with the direction my party had taken over the last few years. I felt as if I and many others had been abandoned as the national Democratic leaders had moved the party farther and farther away from the principles that had once made it great. I mentioned tax cuts, education reform, family values, and a prescription drug benefit under Medicare but stressed most emphatically the war on terror.

This old history professor talked about a frustration with Democratic leaders who had become so eager to defeat George Bush that they did not seem to realize he was acting on the same ideals we Democrats had supported for years: promoting prosperity and equal opportunity, giving help to Americans who need it most, defending America's security and preserving her freedom. I said I was fed up with the politicians "who claim to represent my party but really represent nothing but special interest groups and their own partisan agendas."

I wanted people to know that all Democrats were not like the talking heads they saw "squawking on their TV, attacking the president," that there were a lot of good, honorable Democrats all across America, "even some here in Washington, D.C.," that felt as I did.

I told them that, luckily, Democrats like us have a courageous and honorable leader whom we can be proud to support. "It just so happens that he has a little 'R' next to his name."

I summed up his attributes this way: "President George W. Bush is the leader America has needed over the last three years—and he is the leader America needs for the next four years. He has led America in a time of recession, terrorism, and war. But through it all he has never forgotten his charge to protect our nation's security and promote opportunity for every American. He is guided by the right principles—aided by his strong faith—and I know that my family and the people of my state are more secure with George W. Bush in the White House."

I then turned my attention to the man who had just won the Iowa caucus, the ultimate in liberal litmus tests. "I have also known John Kerry for several years, and I've considered him a friend. He served our country honorably in Vietnam, and he has served our party admirably through much of his tenure in the Senate. But after listening to Senator Kerry over the last year or two—after hearing the agenda he had laid out for our country—I can not support him in his race for the presidency. There are too many issues about which John Kerry and I disagree. And there are too few similarities between John F. Kerry and the great Democratic leaders I've known."

I then tried to explain by asking them to consider one of our greatest Democratic presidents, John Fitzgerald Kennedy, and reminded them that back in 1963 President Kennedy proposed a 13.6-billion-dollar tax cut, which, at the time, was the largest tax cut in history. Part of President Kennedy's plan was to cut the top tax rate by six percentage points, and a lot of Democrats howled with outrage.

President Kennedy had also proposed cutting the lowest tax rate to 14 percent. President Bush went even further and asked us to cut that bottom rate to 10 percent, so that the people who are working hard to make ends meet have a little more breathing room at the end of the month.

All told, President Kennedy's proposed tax cuts equaled more than 2 percent of the national economy. President Bush's proposed tax cuts—the tax cuts some Democrats said would gut the federal government—represented 1.2 percent of the economy.

I summed it up this way: "John F. Kerry may have the same initials as John F. Kennedy, but he has a far different view of what the government should do to help families prosper."

Senator Kerry had made no bones about the fact that he wanted to bring more money into Washington so that he could decide how to spend it. "In his first one hundred days in office, John Kerry's massive health care plan would have forced him to raise taxes by as much as $900 billion. And the only way he's going to get that kind of money is if he reaches into the wallet of every man and woman in America. His spending and tax plan would stifle our economy and stall our recovery."

I had been proud to be the original co-sponsor of President Bush's tax relief plan in the Senate, along with my good friend and fellow born-and-raised Georgian, Senator Phil Gramm of Texas. That bill ultimately sent $1.3 trillion back to the hard-working men and women who earned it.

That tax relief flowed throughout our economy. People used it to pay the bills, get the kids new clothes or start a little savings plan for themselves. Small businesses invested in new equipment and expanded their operations. It had been the main reason our economy began its upswing, making this one of the shortest and shallowest recessions ever.

I also told them that I could remember when most Democrats were in favor of protecting America's power abroad because we believed that "America was a great force for good over evil," and that John Kerry was also out of step with some of the Democratic Party's greatest leaders on foreign policy.

President Harry S. Truman had recognized early on that Communism was a source of evil and a danger to our way of life, and he acted forcefully to meet the threat. In 1946, even before the Soviet threat was clearly evident, he had forced a shutdown with Stalin that pushed the Red Army out of occupied positions in Iran.

In 1947, when Communist insurgents threatened to overthrow the government of Greece, Truman had rallied America and the world, announcing the new Truman Doctrine. He had committed $400 million to protect "free peoples" from "totalitarian regimes."

From 1948 to 1949, President Truman stood down the Soviet blockade of West Berlin not by appeasement but by flying in supplies and saving the city from Soviet encroachment. Thanks to his firm and courageous action, West Berlin then became a beacon of hope and liberty for people in the Eastern Bloc yearning for freedom.

In 1950, President Truman committed U.S. troops to defend South Korea and drive the North Koreans back across the 38th parallel. "While Harry Truman was on the watch, free people everywhere knew they had a friend in the United States of America," I reminded them.

"That was our legacy. For decades, the Democratic Party maintained peace through strength." I also pointed out that Republicans in Congress back then had worked with us to ensure that freedom and democracy would not falter in the face of any threat. "But these days it seems like some people in my party are motivated more by partisan politics than by national interest."

I believed John Kerry had the wrong idea about how our country should respond to the threat of terrorism when he said the war on terror should be "mainly a law enforcement action." I said, "I know that an army of lawyers can be scary sometimes, but surely it doesn't compare to the Army of the United States—not to mention the Marine Corps, the Navy, the Air Force, the Coast Guard, and all of our reservists and the National Guardsmen who are fighting under the flag of the United States of America."

I reminded them that we had tried John Kerry's approach to fighting terror over the last decade. "Is it any wonder that after a decade of weak-willed responses to terror, the terrorists thought we would never fight back?" I asked.

I continued, "I hate that it took the awful tragedy of September 11, 2001, to wake us up to reality. But I'm sure glad we did wake up. And I'm grateful that George W. Bush was leading America exactly when we needed a steel spine and a clear head in the White House."

As far as Kerry's suggestion that the United States should have waited for United Nations diplomats to decide when we could take action in Iraq, rather than standing up for our own right to protect our security and promote democracy, I responded, "I can't imagine the great Democratic Party leaders of past generations waiting with their hands in their pockets while a bunch of dithering diplomats decided the future of the world."

I mentioned the famous quotation of President John F. Kennedy, who told the world, "We shall pay any price, bear any burden, meet any hardship, support any friend, oppose any foe, in order to assure the survival and the success of liberty."

I pointed out that John Kerry had made the right decision when he voted to authorize the war in Iraq. But then he went out on the campaign trail and started spending too much time with Howard Dean. He came back to Washington and voted against the $87 billion the troops needed for protective armor, combat pay, and better health care. I called it "the worst kind of indecisiveness and the wrong leadership at one of the most critical moments in our history."

I ended my remarks by saying that I had been proud to work with President Bush because he shares the same beliefs that support the foundation of my career in public service—and the same ideals that the greatest leaders of the Democratic Party had held for decades.

"I've always believed it's not whose team you're on, it's whose side you're on. In this election, I'm on George Bush's side because he's on the side of the American people. I'm grateful for his service to America, and I'm confident that he'll be reelected in November."

No one would have believed it at the time, and some still may dispute it, but when the votes were all counted on November 2, 2004, a full one-third of the votes President Bush received were from voters who did not identify themselves as Republicans.

Chapter 5

THE KEYNOTE SPEECH

Three weeks before I was to deliver the keynote, I sent my final effort to campaign manager Ken Mehlman and to Ed Walsh, a fine speechwriter who had been extremely helpful with previous remarks. I told them I knew it was too long and would appreciate their help in getting it in the right time frame. It was approximately 3,500 words and I knew it would have to be cut in half. The keynote speech I had delivered in 1992 was 1,400 words. However, I wanted them, rather than me, to cut the speech. A writer often gets prideful of his words; he falls in love with them and finds it hard to throw any of them overboard. But they didn't want to make the cuts either. In fact, they had a few domestic policy lines they wanted me to add.

Later, we also would decide to keep in Kerry's Senate record on national defense. I realized that the Kerry cuts were so deep I'd need detailed documentation to disprove my detractors. We prepared the facts and dates detailing Kerry's abysmal record on national defense, but I had little chance to use it. The media bought the Kerry war room talking points lock, stock, and barrel.

About a week before the convention I was told I had a total of fifteen minutes to give my speech, so I took out the meat ax and started chopping. I tossed a lot of the bipartisan history I had wanted to emphasize, the personal anecdotes of Mama and the mountains and Daddy's coat with the sergeant stripes. Half of it was discarded. What remained was thirteen minutes of slashing-take-no-prisoners red meat. I focused keenly on the Kerry nineteen-year record in the Senate for which my fellow senator had chosen to allot twenty-seven seconds at the Democratic Convention in Boston eight weeks earlier.

On the morning of the speech, as I practiced it on the teleprompter in a rehearsal room set up in the bowels of Madison Square Garden, the suggestion was made that I cut it by another two minutes. I readily agreed, because by now I was living in fear of stealing time from the Cheneys, a couple I respect and love dearly. I sure didn't want to do that, so more went into the wastebasket.

Over and over in my long political speaking career, I've been reminded that television speeches should be conversational. Shirley would always urge me to "talk like you talk to Asia," our granddaughter for whom I've never had a harsh word.

I've listened. I've tried. But I've never been able to do it. You might say it's one of the occupational hazards that comes from a lifetime of traveling the roads of Georgia from Rabun Gap to the Tybee lighthouse. Speaking without amplification from the backs of flatbed trucks, concrete picnic tables, and Coca-Cola crates, I learned fast and early that if you don't speak up, you might as well give up. Five decades and thousands of speeches later, my voice still rises, my eyes flash, the deep scar between my eyes grows deeper, and that well-worn instinct to remove the hide from my opponent takes over. So, Marine recruit Miller marched out onto that stage, stood at attention, and delivered for the drill instructor in my head who bellows, "Speak up, private, I can't hear you."

Zell Miller delivering the Republican National Convention keynote address.

The remarks by Democratic Senator Zell Miller of Georgia at the Republican National Convention:

MILLER: Thank you very much. Since I last stood in this spot, a whole new generation of the Miller family has been born: four great-grandchildren. Along with all the other members of our close-knit family, they are my and Shirley's most precious possessions. And I know that's how you feel about your family, also. Like you, I think of their future, the promises and the perils they will face. Like you, I believe that the next four years will determine what kind of world they will grow up in. And like you, I ask: Which leader is it today that has the vision, the willpower, and, yes, the backbone to best protect my family? (*applause*)

The clear answer to that question has placed me in this hall with you tonight. For my family is more important than my party. (*applause*) There is but one man to whom I am willing to entrust their future, and that man's name is George W. Bush. (*applause*)

In the summer of 1940, I was an eight-year-old boy living in a remote little Appalachian valley. Our country was not yet at war, but even we children knew that there were some crazy men across the ocean who would kill us if they could. President Roosevelt, in a speech that summer, told America, "All private plans, all private lives, have been in a sense repealed by an overriding public danger." In 1940, Wendell Wilkie was the Republican nominee. And there is no better example of someone repealing their "private plans" than this good man. He gave Roosevelt the critical support he needed for a peacetime draft, an unpopular idea at the time. And he made it clear that he would rather lose the election than make national security a partisan campaign issue. (*applause*)

Shortly before Wilkie died, he told a friend that if he could write his own epitaph and had to choose between "here lies a president" or "here lies one who contributed to saving freedom," he would prefer the latter. (*applause*)

Where are such statesmen today? Where is the bipartisanship in this country when we need it most? (*applause*)

Today, at the same time young Americans are dying in the sands of Iraq and the mountains of Afghanistan, our nation is being torn apart and made weaker because of the Democrats' manic obsession to bring down our commander in chief. (*applause*)

What has happened to the party I've spent my life working in? I can remember when Democrats believed that it was the duty of America to fight for freedom over tyranny. It was Democratic president Harry Truman who pushed the Red Army out of Iran, who came to the aid of Greece when Communists threatened to overthrow it, who stared down the Soviet blockade of West Berlin by flying in supplies and saving the city. Time after time in our history, in the face of great danger, Democrats and Republicans worked together to ensure that freedom would not falter. But not today. (*applause*)

Motivated more by partisan politics than by national security, today's Democratic leaders see America as an occupier, not a liberator. And nothing makes this Marine madder than someone calling American troops occupiers rather than liberators. (*applause*)

Tell that to the one-half of Europe that was freed because Franklin Roosevelt led an army of liberators, not occupiers. Tell that to the lower half of the Korean Peninsula that is free because Dwight Eisenhower commanded an army of liberators, not occupiers. Tell that to the half a billion men, women, and children who are free today from Poland to Siberia, because Ronald Reagan rebuilt a military of liberators, not occupiers. (*applause*)

Never in the history of the world has any soldier sacrificed more for the freedom and liberty of total strangers than the American soldier. (*applause*)

And, our soldiers don't just give freedom abroad, they preserve it for us here at home. For it has been said so truthfully that it is the soldier, not the reporter, who has given us the freedom of the press. (*applause*)

It is the soldier, not the poet, who has given us freedom of speech. (*applause*)

It is the soldier, not the agitator, who has given us the freedom to protest. (*applause*)

It is the soldier who salutes the flag, serves beneath the flag, whose coffin is draped by the flag, who gives that protester the freedom he abuses to burn that flag. (*applause*)

No one should dare to even think about being the commander in chief of this country if he doesn't believe with all his heart that our soldiers are liberators abroad and defenders of freedom at home. (*applause*)

But don't waste your breath telling that to the leaders of my party today. In their warped way of thinking, America is the problem, not the solution. They don't believe there is any real danger in the world except that which America brings upon itself through our clumsy and misguided foreign policy.

It is not their patriotism, it is their judgment that has been so sorely lacking. They claimed Carter's pacifism would lead to peace. They were wrong. They claimed Reagan's defense buildup would lead to war. They were wrong. And no pair has been more wrong, more loudly, more often than the two senators from Massachusetts, Ted Kennedy and John Kerry. (*applause*)

Together, Kennedy and Kerry have opposed the very weapons system that won the Cold War and that are now winning the war on terror. Listing all the weapon systems that Senator Kerry tried his best to shut down sounds like an auctioneer selling off our national security. (*audience laughing*)

But Americans need to know the facts. The B-1 bomber, that Senator Kerry opposed, dropped 40 percent of the bombs in the first six months of Enduring Freedom. The B-2 bomber, that Senator Kerry opposed, delivered air strikes against the Taliban in Afghanistan and Hussein's command post in Iraq. (*applause*)

The F-14A Tomcats, that Senator Kerry opposed, shot down Gadhafi's Libyan MiGs over the Gulf of Sidra. (*applause*)

The modernized F-14D, that Senator Kerry opposed, delivered missile strikes against Tora Bora. (*applause*)

The Apache helicopter, that Senator Kerry opposed, took out those Republican Guard tanks in Kuwait in the Gulf War. (*applause*)

The F-15 Eagles, that Senator Kerry opposed, flew cover over our nation's capital and this very city after 9/11. (*applause*)

I could go on and on and on—against the Patriot Missile that shot down Saddam Hussein's scud missiles over Israel; against the Aegis air-defense cruiser; against the Strategic Defense Initiative; against the Trident missile, against, against, against. This is the man who wants to be the commander in chief of our U.S. Armed Forces? U.S. forces armed with what? Spitballs? (*applause*)

Twenty years of votes can tell you much more about a man than twenty weeks of campaign rhetoric. Campaign talk tells people who you want them to think you are. How you vote tells people who you really are deep inside. (*applause*)

Senator Kerry has made it clear that he would use military force only if approved by the United Nations. Kerry would let Paris decide when America needs defending. I want Bush to decide. (*applause*)

John Kerry, who says he doesn't like outsourcing, wants to outsource our national security. That's the most dangerous outsourcing of all. This politician wants to be leader of the free world. Free for how long? For more than twenty years, on every one of the great issues of freedom and security, John Kerry has been more wrong, more weak, and more wobbly than any other national figure. (*applause*)

As a war protester, Kerry blamed our military. As a senator, he voted to weaken our military. And nothing shows that more sadly and more clearly than his vote this year to deny protective armor for our troops in harm's way, far away. (*audience booing*)

George W. Bush understands that we need new strategies to meet new threats. John Kerry wants to re-fight yesterday's war. President Bush believes we have to fight today's war and be ready for tomorrow's challenges. President Bush is committed to providing the kind of forces it takes to root out terrorists, no matter what spider hole they may hide in or what rock they crawl under. (*applause*)

George W. Bush wants to grab terrorists by the throat and not let them go to get a better grip. From John Kerry, they get a "yes/no/maybe" bowl of mush that can only encourage our enemies and confuse our friends. I first got to know George W. Bush when we served as governors together. I admire this man. I am moved by the respect he shows the first lady, his unabashed love for his parents and his daughters . . . (*applause*) . . . and the fact that he is unashamed of his belief that God is not indifferent to America. (*applause*)

I can identify with someone who has lived that line in "Amazing Grace"—"was blind, but now I see." And I like the fact that he's the same man on Saturday night that he is on Sunday morning. (*applause*)

He is not a slick talker but he is a straight shooter. And where I come from, deeds mean a lot more than words. (*applause*)

I have knocked on the door of this man's soul and found someone home, a God-fearing man with a good heart and a spine of tempered steel . . . (*applause*). . . the man I trust to protect my most precious possession: my family. (*applause*)

This election will change forever the course of history, and that's not any history. It's our family's history. The only question is: How? The answer lies with each of us. And like many generations before us, we've got some hard choosing to do. Right now the world just cannot afford an indecisive America. Faint-hearted self-indulgence will put at risk all we care about in this world. In this hour of danger, our president has had the courage to stand up. And this Democrat is proud to stand up with him. (*applause*)

Thank you. God bless this great country. And God bless George W. Bush. (*applause*)

Chapter 6

HARDBALL HUFF

As I headed to the platform overlooking the arena to appear on the television show *Hardball with Chris Matthews*, I was not in the best of moods. One reason was I had always thought that after a major speech, I'd let the speech speak for itself in that first news cycle. Interviews only detract from a speech and, in most cases, step on your message and end up becoming the story. However, the folks in whose hands I had placed myself for four busy days thought differently; they wanted me on the show, and I was trying to do as they wished.

My first impression of Chris Matthews had been in the mid-seventies when he was a brash young man in a hurry writing speeches for President Jimmy Carter. Later, I had loved his book *Hardball* and had given it to several friends as a present.

But since being in the Senate, I had come to detest Chris Matthews's know-it-all attitude and his bullying way of interviewing, especially when he had the person by remote and not in the same studio. To make matters worse, I had something else stuck in my craw. Earlier that evening, in the time leading up to the speech, when the pundits were pontificating at full throttle, Ron Reagan, who had covered dog shows before he became a scientific marvel in stem cell research, out of the clear blue sky, said, "I've always thought of Miller as sort of weird, you know," and asked Matthews about me. Matthews answered him with the curt observation that I was "an old time seggy" (segregationist). Howard Fineman of *Newsweek* then chirped up, "He wasn't really quite a Democrat in 1992 when he was lured into supporting Clinton by James Carville." What? It was I who had introduced Carville to Clinton, not the other way around, as Fineman's twisted thinking had it.

Also, all the civil rights leaders of Atlanta had been a key part of my eight campaigns for statewide offices. As governor I had appointed more African Americans to judgeships and boards than all the other governors together, including the one from Plains for whom Matthews had once worked. I had appointed the only African American attorney general in the nation.

So with this group to face, I took a deep breath, looked into the camera, heard the loud booing from Herald Square where this open-minded, informed, and objective panel was set up, and waited for the interview to go downhill. It did not take long, for my always short fuse was already spewing.

Matthews started off by demanding to know again and again if I really believed John Kerry and Ted Kennedy wanted to defend America with spitballs. I attempted to explain Kerry's record, the vote against $87 billion for our troops in Iraq and his efforts to cancel the M.X. missile, the B-1 bomber, the anti-satellite system and other military programs critical to our national defense. I explained that the "spitballs" comment was a metaphor. But Matthews was only interested in his usual liberal bias and rapid-fire questions. He wanted to know if I was in favor of starving little kids, ending education and killing old people. I tried to restrain myself by returning to the issues and facts at hand. I wanted viewers to learn and remember the facts. But Matthews's lack of hospitality pushed this old Marine too far, and, on a steady rotation in the 24/7 news cycle, viewers heard this:

MATTHEWS: Well, it's a tough question. It takes a few
    words.
MILLER: Get out of my face. If you are going to ask me a
    question, step back and let me answer.
MATTHEWS: Senator, please.
MILLER: You know, I wish we . . . I wish we lived in the
    day where you could challenge a person to a duel.

The only upside to the interview was when J.C. Watts came on at the end and offered, "Hey, Senator, this is J.C. Watts."

Thanks goodness, I thought, finally a kindred spirit. "Hey, J.C.," I responded, overwhelmed by anger, frustration and a bit of self-contempt.

"You can put your feet under my dinner table any day of the week," Watts obliged.

Overall the interview had not gone well. It was not pretty. I regret it. What made it worse for me was that I had taken my fifteen-year-old grandson, Bryan Miller, to New York to be with his "Pa-pa" on the big night. I can only imagine what he must have felt and how he will remember it.

Early the next morning, I was to appear on *Imus in the Morning*. If you still doubt there's a liberal bias in the media, consider this: Don Imus publicly identified himself as a Kerry supporter on his morning show, and still he was able to conduct a decent and polite interview when compared to the "objective" and "unbiased" likes of Chris Matthews. In fact, Imus himself called Matthews's questions of me from the night before "idiotic" and "out of line."

The day after the speech and the *Hardball* debacle, *Congressional Quarterly Today* reported that White House Chief of Staff Andrew H. Card "found himself on the defensive about Democratic Senator Zell Miller's keynote address at the Republican Convention, which was so angry and bitter that some analysts are suggesting it might backfire."

"Republicans thought they had scored a coup by getting Miller, who delivered one of the keynote addresses at the Democratic Convention in New York twelve years ago, to play the same role here," the article continued. "But the Georgian's attacks on his fellow senator, the Democratic nominee of Massachusetts, were so furious—delivered with his face contorted with anger—that analysts are already comparing it to Pat Buchanan's disastrous speech to the 1992 Republican Convention. That speech included references to a 'cultural war' that made the GOP look like a hate-filled party to some voters."

Card replied, "I think he delivered the speech that Zell Miller wanted the country to hear. He kind of tells it like it is." The reporters somehow interpreted that as "putting some pointed distance" between myself and President Bush.

Kerry campaign manager Mary Beth Cahill came forth and proclaimed: "I think Zell Miller will be the lasting impression. People remember gasoline."

But when asked in a *USA Today* interview, the day after the speech, if I had scared off undecided voters, Karl Rove replied, "No I think it's going to be widely and favorably received. . . . The fact that he is angry as a Democrat about what has happened in the Democratic Party and he is upset with the views and votes and statements of fellow Democratic senators gives his speech enormous credibility and makes it a very persuasive case for this president."

But there were many reporters who were calling it an "over the top" performance. One wrote that I had been selected to make waves but instead "unleashed a tsunami." Copies of *Roget's Thesaurus* were dragged off the shelf by reporters to find more and more descriptive words for "angry" and "crazy." Later, my home state newspaper, the *Atlanta Journal–Constitution*, would gleefully report that "crazy" had been used to describe me more than 100,000 times according to a Google search.

Pollster John Zogby gave his opinion that the speech was "too hot" for undecided voters. But another pollster, Frank Luntz, was conducting a focus group in Ohio during the speech with swing voters and after the speech asked which presidential contender would be more likely to change his mind on an issue. Sixteen of seventeen picked Kerry. Luntz explained further: "the attack on Kerry resonated because Miller anchored his criticism with specific argument." The members of the group described the speech as "fantastic," "very upbeat," "energetic," "powerful but one-sided," "intellectual," "dynamic," and "on target." Only one woman said I was "totally overboard."

Kathleen Parker, a columnist for the *Orlando Sentinel*, wrote, "If there were any Bubbas undecided before Miller, there aren't anymore. You can bet your duckblind on that."

John Harvard of the *Wall Street Journal* said I looked "like the spouse in a divorce proceeding who says, and, oh yeah, she's a child molester too."

John Podhoretz, columnist of the *New York Post*, wrote, "It was astonishingly harsh. . .in a way that no major Republican politician would dare to be." His colleague Stefan C. Friedman called the speech "a white hot attack."

Craig Crawford, a columnist for *Congressional Quarterly*, wrote, "Miller's turncoat GOP performance, bordering on demonic hysteria, made it a good night for Howard Dean. He is no longer the craziest-sounding Democrat on the planet. Who needs the Dean Scream when you've got the Zell Yell?"

Dan Baltz of the *Washington Post* called the speech "one of the most biting and personal attacks ever delivered at a modern-day presidential convention."

His colleague Lisa de Moras took exception to the line in the speech that "the soldier, not the reporter, has given us freedom of speech," saying that "Miller can make the word 'reporter' sound like a dirty word." Huh? I wonder what she and her ilk make the word "soldier" sound like? This same objective member of the Fourth

49

Estate also wrote that the day after the speech I "was roaming around Madison Square Garden like a rabid dog looking for someone else to bite."

It seems as if every reporter, columnist, and janitor at the *Washington Post* got in their licks. Harold Meyerson deemed the speech "a crazed sermon. . .surpassing in its malice and mendacity even the Swift Boat ads. . .delivered with the monomaniacal intensity of an ancient prelate condemning heretics to the stake."

A similar comparison to witch-burning came from *New York Times* columnist Maureen Dowd, who thought the speaking podium looked like a "cross" and I was "Cotton Mather behind the cross."

USA Today called the speech "fire-breathing," while the *San Francisco Chronicle* said I went off "like a Roman candle," and the *Philadelphia News* called it "a scorching, almost biblical diatribe."

The Fresco (CA) Bee called the speech "an angry broadside" with "impassioned fusillades," and later suggested that on leaving the Senate I should start my own show on the *Discovery Channel* called *In Search of Marbles.*

The *Phoenix New Times* said I was "mean as a junk yard dog on a four foot leash." The *Palestine Chronicle* called the speech "Rove speak," while Bill McClellan of the *St. Louis Post-Dispatch* thought it "an odd combination of God and Glocks."

Vincent Flore of the *Washington Dispatch* wrote that I was "possibly hated now by Democrats more than Ken Starr." *Time* called me "the convention's prime pit bull turncoat" and said that I "made Dick Cheney seem warm and fuzzy."

The *Wall Street Journal's* Al Hunt simply got it wrong. He said, "Miller was passionate when he was a racist thirty years ago." Never mind that thirty years ago I was elected lieutenant governor of Georgia with the endorsement and active support of Coretta Scott King, John Lewis, Julian Bond, Andrew Young, Maynard Jackson, and a host of other civil rights leaders. A young volunteer in my campaign office at that time was Shirley Franklin, who is now the dynamic mayor of Atlanta.

Wrong also was the *Pittsburgh Post-Gazette*, calling me a "veteran huckster" who started my career as "lieutenant governor to racist Lester Maddox." For the record, at one time earlier in my career I had worked for three governors in a row: Carl Sanders, Lester Maddox, and then Jimmy Carter, in that order. But I was lieutenant governor under Governor George Busbee, not Lester Maddox, and we both were supported by all of the respected civil rights leaders of Atlanta.

The *New York Daily News*, looking ahead at getting out the vote, used this ominous threat: "Any Democrat who doesn't vote this time ought to be dropped into a vat of donkey manure [and] be forced to watch an endless loop of Zell Miller's speech at the GOP convention."

Offering its advice to our Republican nominee, the *Duluth News Tribune* suggested that the president would do well to "distance himself from the acostic, over-the-top support of a sad, distrusting elder who has lost his statesmanship" and later reported that my mental stability should be questioned, "the manic of Miller's outburst was an invitation to an asylum."

Daniel Ruth of the *Tampa Tribune*, referring to me as "Dr. Strangelove," wrote that "had [Zell] gone on much longer you might have expected him to start babbling about how a vote for George W. Bush is a vote to protect the purity of our national fluids . . .This was the paranoid sermon just before they start handing out the Kool-Aid. . .it was Elmer Gantry on speed. . .It was Hannibal meets *Deliverance*. It was Gomer Pyle meets *Full Metal Jacket*, a fulminating Foghorn Leghorn meets *The Passion of the Christ* . . .who sought to portray Kerry as the concubine of Beelzebub."

Pollster Frank Luntz even topped that. He told *The Hill* that "Hitler does better among Jewish voters than Zell Miller does with Democrats."

Not all of the U.S. newspaper reviews were so biting and negative, however. The *Boston Herald* editorialized that I spoke "for a significant segment of the Democratic Party that feels abandoned, one that the John Kerry wing doesn't understand and makes no effort to court." They continued, "the retiring U.S. senator from Georgia is, of course, at a point in his life when he can darned well do and say anything he wants to—and last night he did."

Similarly, the *Kansas City Star* said of the speech, "the applause and noise were as loud as they have been all week [of the RNC Convention]," while Paul Brownfield, of the *Los Angeles Times*, said that "Miller's speech, love it or hate it, had what TV demands—personality."

Peter Washington of the *Toronto Sun* had this to say: "[Miller's] speech was one that hasn't been matched since Ronald Reagan's mesmerizing speech in 1964—40 years ago—that excited Republicans all the way to the White House. While Reagan's 1964 speech was tough and forceful, it was also quiet and measured—none of the righteous outrage of Zell Miller's tirade about the disaster he thinks John Kerry would be for the military and America. What is so significant about Miller's speech is that it wasn't aimed at Republicans but Americans of all political leanings . . .There were no pauses for orchestrated applause. . .It's barely within living memory since such a speech has been made at a convention."

In an editorial in the *Kansas City Star* titled "Zell's Anger Echoes Here," it was written that "Zell Miller is walking away from the Senate too soon. I fear we'll not see his like again."

And Tim Goodman of the *San Francisco Chronicle* wrote that "somewhere this very morning, in a Democratic strategy session, someone is probably saying this: 'Well, here's an idea, guys. How about not making Zell Miller mad again?'"

Following the lead of most of their U.S. counterparts, the European press began to pile on. The *Telegraph* in London: "Speaking with a fixed scowl and using flat southern vowels, Miller launched an attack on Mr. Kerry so savage that it drew gasps of shock and approval from the delegates. One by one, he listed the 10 weapons systems he said that Mr. Kerry had voted against during his Senate career and which were now needed in the war against terror.

The worst sin of all was Mr. Kerry's muted attachment to working with the United Nations. Kerry would let Paris decide when America needs defending, Mr. Miller spat, perhaps the ultimate sand in the eyes of Republican activists in the post-September 11 era."

The *Telegraph* further saw the speech this way: "Bush campaign staff knew of those risks when they handed Mr. Miller a prized prime-time speaking slot. That is a measure of the Republicans' confidence that they can destroy their opponent in the next two months and an indication of the scale of the challenge Mr. Kerry now faces." The article also noted, "That was a homerun, muttered one Army veteran as Mr. Miller left the stage to thunderous applause."

The *Financial Times (London)* called it an "angry, vitriolic speech [which] as good as accused John Kerry and his party of being gutless, godless pinkos under the thumb of France." The paper also described me this way: "eyes bulging and teeth bared, [Miller] unleashed one of the most vicious attacks in the history of conventions." Another reporter with the *Financial Times* called me a "wild-eyed Democrat party apostle. Like General Grant, he takes the fight to the enemy."

"Sounding like Jed Clampett from *The Beverly Hillbillies*, the white-haired ex-Marine lambasted Democrats," the *London Daily Mail* opined. "It was amazing behavior. Yet Miller's hard-edged rhetoric turned a majority of independent voters who watched it in a focus group exercise into Bush supporters straight away." The article continued, "His speech sent out a terrifying message to the Kerry team: Bush and his handlers don't simply want to pull ahead in the final 60 days, they want to destroy you with a Reagan-style landslide."

Back in the U.S., television talking heads also got into the game. Tim Russert of NBC called the speech "one of the strongest-worded speeches I've ever heard at a convention." NBC's Andrea Mitchell said it was "more than a red meat speech. It was a raw meat speech." CBS's Dan Rather said that I "stroked passions" and stirred delegates to boo at John Kerry's name. NBC's Tom Brokaw said that I "lit up these delegates with some very tough language." The *New York Times*'s David Brooks said on ABC's *Nightline*, "It was prosecution night and Zell Miller delivered a stem-winder that was like Harry Truman giving 'em hell." ABC's George Stephanopoulos wondered if it was smart to have me "out there in such a hot fashion."

MSNBC's David Gregory said on *Hardball* that he had said to Governor Benson of New Hampshire that, "yes, it might have been tough. It even seemed over the top. But its the kind of thing that's really going to motivate not just the base but the workers in ... these swing states that have to get out the vote. That's what's going to decide the election. These kinds of speeches have got people pumped up now."

One of the "Beltway Boys" on Fox, Morton Kondracke, weighed in: "I thought that Zell Miller went over the line into demagoguery, frankly, when he implied that the Democrats are defaming American troops and have been doing so during the Cold War and the Korean War by declaring them to be occupiers and not liberators. That is something that Democrats have not done."

Several commentators shared Kondracke's opinion that no Democrat had called our soldiers "occupiers" rather than "liberators," as I had charged. Really? The two longest-serving senators in the U.S. Senate, Robert Byrd and Ted Kennedy, both did. Senator Kennedy had earlier said, "To the people in the Middle East the symbol of America is not the Statue of Liberty," while Byrd said, referring to President Bush: "Our emperor says that we are not occupiers, yet we show no inclination to relinquish the country of Iraq to its people."

Even fake news anchor Jon Stewart of *The Daily Show* on Comedy Central took his shots. In a segment titled "Zell on Earth," Stewart said that I had "used the convention's prime speaking spot to issue an angry tirade against John Kerry, the Democratic Party, and anybody else in spittle range."

Fellow political figures also had their say. Iowa governor Tom Vilsack warned in a *Washington Post* interview that "anger doesn't sell well in my neck of the woods." Vice-presidential candidate John Edwards said the speech made him mad. My Senate colleague John McCain said the speech "makes Buchanan's 1992 speech. . .look like milquetoast" and added that he thought it would "backfire."

But the crowning blow came from President Jimmy Carter, who sent me this letter after first giving it to the press.

To Senator Zell Miller:

You seem to have forgotten that loyal Democrats elected you as mayor and as state senator. Loyal Democrats, including members of my family and me, elected you as lieutenant governor and as governor. It was a loyal Democrat, Lester Maddox, who assigned you to high positions in the state government when you were out of office. It was a loyal Democrat, Roy Barnes, who appointed you as U.S. Senator when you were out of office. By your historically unprecedented disloyalty, you have betrayed our trust.

Great Georgia Democrats who served in the past, including Walter George, Richard Russell, Herman Talmadge, and Sam Nunn disagreed strongly with the policies of Franklin Roosevelt, Harry Truman, John Kennedy, and me, but they maintained their loyalty to the party in which they gained their public office. Other Democrats, because of philosophical differences or the race issue, like Bo Callaway and Strom Thurmond, at least had the decency to become Republicans.

Everyone knows that you were chosen to speak at the Republican Convention because of your being a "Democrat," and it's quite possible that your rabid and mean-spirited speech damaged our party and paid the Republicans some transient dividends.

Perhaps most troublesome of all is seeing you adopt an established and very effective Republican campaign technique of destroying the character of opponents by

Talking with President Jimmy Carter in the Oval Office.

wild and false allegations. The Bush campaign's personal attacks on the character of John McCain in South Carolina in 2000 was a vivid example. The claim that war hero Max Cleland was a disloyal American and an ally of Osama Bin Laden should have given you pause, but you have joined in this ploy by your bizarre claims that another war hero, John Kerry, would not defend the security of our nation except with spitballs. (This is the same man whom you described previously as "one of this nation's authentic heroes, one of the party's best-known and greatest leaders—and a good friend.")

I myself never claimed to have been a war hero, but I served in the Navy from 1942 to 1953, and as president, greatly strengthened our military forces and protected our nation and its interests in every way. I don't believe this warrants your referring to me as a pacifist.

Zell, I have known you for forty-two years and have, in the past, respected you as a trustworthy political leader and a personal friend. But now, there are many of us loyal Democrats who feel uncomfortable in seeing that you have chosen the rich over the poor, unilateral preemptive war over a strong nation united with others for peace, lies and obfuscation over the truth, and the political technique of personal character assassination as a way to win elections or to garner a few moments of applause. These are not the characteristics of great Democrats whose legacy you and I have inherited.

Sincerely, and with deepest regrets,
Jimmy

Georgian Kay Reed, the editor of the *Albany Herald* who has covered me for decades, saw it a different way,

Zell Miller's keynote . . . could have been entitled, "A Marine goes to Congress" or "A Mountain Boy Goes to

Washington." Miller has been a loyal Democrat through four decades in public office . . . he stood by members of his party through thick and thin. He was the Georgia Democrats standard bearer, the model for young members of the party . . . . But arriving in Congress, something happened. He no longer was charged with looking after the affairs of just his state and its people. He gained a view of the whole world and a new perspective in priorities. He also saw from the inside that Democrats in Congress had their focus on their party—sometimes at the expense of the nation's interest. . . . Age does have its advantages. It gives the long view with the benefit of vast experiences. Since going to Washington, Miller began looking at his children, grandchildren, and great-grand-children as a guide to what America's priorities should be. . . . What television viewers heard and saw was brutal honesty from a politician who had realized that loyalty to a party should not come before loyalty to country. . . . He's the same Zell Georgians have always known. The difference is he's been to Washington.

Barack Obama, the Democratic keynoter, made one of the best speeches I've ever heard made anywhere. It caught the attention of everyone, as well it should have. I've met this impressive young man who has an unlimited future ahead of him. But whether he did the job a keynoter must do will long be debated. For as the veteran CNN analyst Jeff Greenfield so aptly put it the night of my speech, I gave a "throwback to the kind of speeches" that once were routine for the keynoter who "was supposed to come out and basically beat the other party upside the head."

However one might see the good, the bad, and the ugly of the speech, I think you could say I fulfilled that role.

Chapter 7

STUMPING FOR THE PRESIDENT

After the RNC in New York, I returned to Georgia a depressed and dejected human being, worried sick that the speech and my outburst with Chris Matthews had done more harm than good to the cause I believed in and the good and courageous man I had wanted to help.

The only smile I was able to muster was when I saw that CNBC had run an online poll and asked, "Who would win the duel?" The response was 86 percent for Miller to 14 percent for Matthews.

I got back home Friday afternoon, and first thing took my yellow Labs, Gus and Woodrow, for a three-mile walk. No matter how hard the winds may blow on the other side of those mountains, when I'm in that Brasstown Valley walking those familiar mountain trails, darkness turns to light and I feel better.

It has always been my sanctuary, but this time it did not help much. The dogs and I took another long walk on Saturday morning, and after returning we laid together in what Shirley calls a "dog pile" on the living room floor. Suddenly, the phone rang and my fortress from the outside world was shattered. It was Ken Mehlman, President Bush's campaign manager who had been traveling with the president. His first words were, "You could run for mayor in Cedar Rapids." If I had not already been in a prone position on the floor, that comment would have knocked me there.

Ken went on to tell me that whenever and wherever the president had mentioned my name, it had been greeted with loud and sustained cheers. All I could say was, "I can't believe it." "Believe it," he answered and said that as soon as possible they'd like for me to travel with the president and also make campaign appearances on my own. The only thing I could think to say was my standard, "I'll do whatever you think will help. I just don't want to hurt."

On Monday, I finally made the effort to check on what the pundits were writing about the post-convention tour. The *New York Times* first reminded the readers that Democratic National Chairman Terry McAuliffe had said that I "was so frightening that parents took their children away from the television." The story then followed with this paragraph, "The crowd in Parkersburg had included the city's mayor, Jimmy Colombo, a Democrat, and the president had told them, 'I think ol' Zell Miller set a pretty good tempo for Democrats all across the country. He made it clear it's all right to come and support the Bush ticket.'"

There was more analysis in the article. "In the hours and days after Mr. Miller's appearance at the convention, Democrats predicted that his speech would backfire by providing evidence that Mr. Bush's campaign was all about attacking Mr. Kerry, . . . his patriotism and scaring voters into the arms of the Republicans. But Mr. Bush's aides said the response to the president's mentions of Mr. Miller showed that Mr. Miller had touched a chord among voters of all stripes by voicing doubts about Mr. Kerry's record on national security issues."

The *Washington Post* reported from Broadview Heights, Ohio, suburb of Cleveland, that it was "Bush's new applause line." At an earlier stop in Kirkland, Bush had said, "There's a lot of folks like Zell. He represents a lot of folks who understand that with four more years, Dick Cheney and I will make this country stronger, safer, and better."

Time reported that there had been a significant post-convention jump of 11 points, 52-41.

The next week I was with the president on a bus tour beginning at Huntington, West Virginia, and then moving into Ohio along the Ohio River, Portsmouth, Irontown, and Chillicothe. It was Appalachian country, and I felt at home with these folks. It was a beautiful fall day.

At the first stop, there were six thousand crammed into the Big Sandy Superstore Arena near Marshall University. Their mascot is called the Herd. Listening to the blaring music and sign-waving crowd, the president had cracked, "By the sound of this, the Herd is thundering."

I presented the president to the revved up crowd this way:

> Thank you very much. I'm proud to be back on the trail with President Bush. As I said at my convention speech in New York, this election will change forever the course of history. And that's not any history; it's our family's history.
>
> There is one man I trust to keep my family safe from terrorists bent on destroying America. One man with the strength to make tough choices when the pressure is high. One man with the resolve to make up his mind and stick with his decisions. One man who will stay on the offensive, never wavering, never wobbling, never weak in the knees. That man is George W. Bush.
>
> I wish my party had the same will to win this fight that our president does. But I thank God George W. Bush is America's leader when America needs strong leadership the most.
>
> And I want to tell all my fellow Democrats—all of you who may never have thought about voting for a Republican before—all of you who might be a little embarrassed to bring it up at the dinner table or to

mention it at a union meeting—that George W. Bush is a Republican we Democrats can proudly support.

In this hour of danger our president has the courage to stand strong, and I'm proud to stand with him.

Ladies and gentlemen, the President of the United States, George W. Bush.

As we made our way into Ohio, crowds were lined up on both sides of the road. Some had brought lawn chairs, many were jumping up and down, and some held small children in their arms. They were enthusiastic, and the president, standing in the doorway of the bus with a bullhorn, always had something to say as the bus slowly navigated its way through the narrow streets.

Many supporters had their dogs with them, and the dog-loving president would always have something to say to them, like "nice dog."

We stopped in the little town of Irontown, where the mayor presented President Bush a key to the city as two thousand people packed in the little town square yelled their support. This was Scioto County, which Bush had carried in 2000 after it had gone for Clinton in the two previous elections.

In Portsmouth at the athletic center of Shawnee State University, I presented the president again, and he began: "This part of the world is like parts of Georgia and parts of Texas where there's a lot of what we call 'discerning Democrats.' That's what Zell was saying—it's OK if you're a Democrat to pull the Bush-Cheney lever."

We continued on and found more than fifteen thousand waiting at the Ross County Fairgrounds in Chillicothe. Congressman Bob Ney introduced me and then, as before, I brought on the president. It was an added treat to spend time with Anthony Munoz, the great NFL Hall of Fame football player who was the Bush-Cheney honorary chairman for Ohio. He was a nice man and very impressive, and I thought about him and Chairman Bob Bennett and all the other great people I had met in that key state when the final Ohio numbers came in on election night.

Ken Mehlman had not exaggerated. Any depression and disappointment I had about the keynote was put to rest. I had seen for myself one of the truisms of politics: For every opponent that is strongly against you, there is a supporter who is just as strongly for you. I had learned and relearned that lesson over the years in smaller ways. I am a person who feels things strongly; I express myself sharply; there is no lukewarm on my thermostat. And I both pay for it and get the benefit from this personality trait.

A few days later, Ken asked me to block out days I would be willing to go alone to swing states, speaking at rallies, visiting local headquarters, and firing up the troops who would later make the difference on Election Day. For the first time I saw this operation up close and witnessed the loyalty and dedication and unbelievable detail that was going into these amazing operations. I always came away more inspired by them than they by me.

I was pinpointed into areas that had once been solidly Democratic and still had more registered Democrats than Republicans. But they were conservative Democrats like me who had seen the party leave us on the cultural issues that were so important, and they were patriots who stood with the president on national security. They were, therefore, potential Bush voters. A good example was the Fourth Congressional District of Pennsylvania, once one of this country's great industrial areas, steel country on the outskirts of Pittsburgh.

I went to Beaver Falls, where Joe Namath played high school football before going on to the University of Alabama and then to the New York Jets and his life as "Broadway Joe." Unbelievably, this southwestern corner of Pennsylvania also produced Joe Montana, Dan Marino, and Jim Kelly, football legends all. But it was politics, not football that was on the minds in the packed high school auditorium. Congresswoman Melissa Hart, a hard-charging conservative who represents the area, introduced me to her delightful mother and to the crowd.

The October journey would take me into more than thirty cities in states as far west as New Mexico, as far north as Lewiston, Maine, Derry, New Hampshire, Duluth, Minnesota, Green Bay, Wisconsin, and as far south as Miami, Florida.

Four days before the election, I was back with the president on Air Force One, going into Pennsylvania once again for Bush's forty-second time. This time it was at a rally of twenty thousand supporters at the Lancaster Airport. Mrs. Bush was along, and it would be the first of four events that day, later stopping at Lima and Youngstown, Ohio, and finally ending up at Pontiac, Michigan.

Lancaster County is the heart of Amish country. Usually, these good and hard-working people are reluctant to get heavily involved in politics, disliking taxes and having a healthy distrust of government. This time seemed to be different, and much of their leadership had come to the airport for a meeting with the president. It was also an area with a large segment of Democrats with social values, and the president took direct aim at the "discerning Democrats," as he would later at the Ohio stops. "If you're a Democrat," he said, "and your dreams and goals are not found in the far left wing of the Democratic Party, I'd be honored to have your vote." He told them he remembered "the strong conscience of the late Democratic governor of Pennsylvania Robert Casey, who once said, 'When we look to the unborn child the real issue is not when life begins, but when love begins.'" The president added that he wanted to move "the nation toward a culture of life. . . . I hope people who usually vote for the other party will take a close look at my agenda."

Throughout the day he reminded audiences that the election had come down to three "clear choices for families—family security, the family wallet, and a family's quality of life. . . . If you are a Democrat who wants to protect marriage from activist judges, then I will be happy to have your vote." Karl Rove made no bones about it: "We're here to make an explicit appeal for the support of Democrats and Independents."

I was in the panhandle of Florida the eve before Election Day with the great NASCAR driver Bobby Labonte. We had hit Fort Myers earlier and then had come on to Escambia County, a county that had given Bush 65 percent of their vote in 2000. Their goal was to increase that to 75 percent in 2004. (It would be closer to 85 percent.) The Democrats knew how crucial this area was, and John Edwards would arrive in Pensacola as we were leaving. This happened frequently throughout the campaign. Edwards and I had been in Saginaw, Michigan, at the same hour and in Council Bluffs, Iowa, former Georgia senator Max Cleland, an old friend, was there within hours of the Bush rally where I spoke.

Pensacola is the largest city in Escambia County, and Bobby and I could see the blue tarpaulins on the roofs of nearly every building as we flew in. The evidence of Hurricane Ivan was still painfully visible. The headquarters where the rally was held was packed to the walls and overflowed into the parking lot. Dozens of volunteers of all ages were working the phone bank. Some creative craftsman had made spitball jewelry. There were necklaces for the women and pins for the men's lapels. I have one of each, which I will always treasure.

We left very upbeat, Bobby on his way to Las Vegas for a car show and I back home for the next day's election. I had a strong premonition, a good feeling that Bush-Cheney would carry Florida and Ohio. I had spent several days in Ohio, from one end of the state to the other, twice in Youngstown where the dynamic Democratic mayor George McKelvey had endorsed the president a few days before the convention in New York. Twice, I was in Toledo, once with the Sean Hannity Get Out the Vote Tour along with J. C. Watts and William Bennett. That was a lot of fun. There were huge crowds, and Jerry Falwell joined us in Erie, Pennsylvania. During an earlier visit to Toledo, I had spent time in the Toledo headquarters that was alive with activity. I'll never forget one of their youngest volunteers, a young man who must have been in his early teens who had done so much work they had dubbed him "Kid Toledo." These indispensable workers are always either the goats or the conquering heroes of a campaign. In Ohio, they were the ones who made the difference in that "must-win" state.

After the election, Steve Bouchard, director of ACT Ohio, who was responsible for getting the Democratic vote out, was interviewed by Matt Bell in a telling analysis in the *New York Times*. He called the day after the election a "rude awakening" and added, "I always thought that there was more of us out there. And this time there was more of them." Were there ever! The ten counties in Ohio with the highest turnout percentages (all more than 75 percent) went for Bush.

I had returned home that Monday night before the election feeling more confident about the election's outcome than at any time during the campaign. I was confident we would carry both Ohio and Florida, and that would assure the victory. Just as I had predicted in 2003, the Democratic campaign had early on completely written off the South.

I did not mention my confidence to Shirley, being the superstitious person that I am. But before going to bed that night, I listed on a sheet of paper the swing states and how I thought each would come out. I sealed my list in an envelope and placed it in a drawer next to my bed. I was right on all of them except Michigan. I had high hopes for an upset victory there after a visit to McComb County, the well-known home of "Reagan Democrats" outside Detroit. I had also been in Saginaw and then with the president at the Silverdome in Pontiac where thirty thousand wildly enthusiastic supporters waving "W" signs greeted the president and the first lady. Also Congresswoman Candice Miller's superb leadership had pushed me into becoming a believer that it could be done in Michigan.

Shirley and I watched the election returns from our living room in that comfortable "dog pile" by the fireplace. At eleven o'clock I still felt confident about the outcome and we moved to our bedroom. When Tom Brokaw at one o'clock in the morning colored Ohio red and said, "It is hard to see how George W. Bush is not reelected president of the United States," I went to the refrigerator and got two Ensures out, a vanilla for Shirley and a chocolate for me. We toasted our newly reelected president, hugged each other, and tried to sleep. We could not sleep, and soon I turned the television back on and continued to savor this sweet victory—in many ways with more pride and happiness than any of my own. The reason was that it was more important than any of my own victories. I had not exaggerated when over and over I had called this election the most important of my lifetime. I'll try to explain why in the following chapter.

Following is the stump speech I gave in varying degrees at all those stops and rallies around the country:

> This old Democrat got to make a speech at the Republican Convention a couple of weeks ago in New York City. And all the political pundits and talking heads said that I looked mad and sounded angry. How very perceptive of them!
>
> As I said in that convention speech, this election, only weeks away, will change forever the course of history. And that's not any history, it's our family's history.
>
> And in this most dangerous time, there is but one man I trust to keep my family safe from terrorists bent on killing Americans. One man with the strength to make tough choices when the pressure is high.
>
> One man with the resolve to make up his mind and stick with his decisions. One man who I know will never waver, never wobble, never get weak in the knees. That man is George W. Bush.
>
> I wish the leaders of my party had the same will to win this fight that our president does. But I thank God George W. Bush is America's leader when America needs strong leadership the most.

I know both these men who are running for president. Served as governors together with George Bush. Served as senators together with John Kerry. They are not made from the same substance. Their fabric and their thinking are as different as night and day. And during the course of this speech, I'll point out some of those differences.

When the president came to office the economy was already taking a turn for the worse. Job growth was slowing down. The stock markets were moving in the wrong direction. Strong medicine was needed.

The first dose was a tax relief plan designed to jump start our economy by getting money out of Washington, D.C., and into the pockets of workers and the small business owners who earned it.

Every dollar spent by government comes from the pocket of working Americans. Those of us in office must never forget that. And you must never let us forget it.

I was proud to be a co-sponsor of those tax relief plans which lowered the tax bills for 111 million taxpayers—including 25 million small business owners.

We've now had *eleven* consecutive quarters of economic growth.

Nearly 1.7 million jobs have been created since last August; we've got to do more and more are on the way. Home ownership is the highest ever.

George W. Bush has done an outstanding job shepherding our economy through the toughest of times. Keep in mind that more than a million jobs were lost in three months after 9/11.

On the other hand, John Kerry's entire plan for the economy can be summed up in four words: tax, spend, redistribute income. Kerry believes that if you rob Peter to pay Paul, Paul will vote for you.

This economy recovery has been spurred on by lower taxes. Kerry's higher taxes, $900 billion the first year, would stifle economic growth and take money out of people's pockets at the worst possible time.

You know, we once had a candidate who said he wanted to "feel your pain." Now, we've got a candidate who wants to "steal your gain."

The differences between Bush and Kerry on foreign policy are just as different as they are on domestic policy. For years, terrorists had been killing Americans and striking at American interests around the world. Each and every attack was met with a totally inadequate and down-right wimpy response.

It was if we had been sending terrorists an engraved invitation to attack us.

After they saw how we did not respond in 1993 after the first World Trade Center bombing, and the Kohbar Towers and then the embassies in Africa and the *U.S.S. Cole*, is it any wonder that the terrorists thought America would never fight back?

America was blessed that George W. Bush was leading America exactly when we most needed a steel spine in the White House.

President Bush immediately took the fight to the terrorists, cleared out their base of operations in Afghanistan, and captured their biggest fan cowering in a spider hole in Iraq.

The president recognized that at a time when terror-ists were growing bolder, we had to change the way the government fights the terrorist threat.

He created the Homeland Security Department, and it was not easy. Even after terrorists had killed our citizens on our own soil, the democratic leadership in the Senate was more concerned about protecting old union rules than giving the president the authority to respond to a national emergency.

I signed on immediately, and for 11 votes, over a period 112 days, I was the lone Democrat to stand with the president. The other Democrats, including Senators John Kerry and John Edwards, stalled it for four long months—at a critical moment for America's security.

But President Bush hung tough and finally, after the 2002 election, after two Democratic senators were defeated, he won approval of the Homeland Security Department.

I also supported President Bush in the war to overthrow Saddam Hussein. And I told this true story to my senate colleagues.

I was doing some work in my back porch in Young Harris, Georgia, tearing out a section of old stacked rocks, when all of a sudden, I uncovered a nest of copperhead snakes. Now, as you may know, a copperhead is poisonous; it will kill you. It could kill one of my grandchildren. It could kill one of my four great-grandchildren who play around there all the time. And, you know, when I discovered those copperheads, I didn't call my wife Shirley, like I do about everything else. I didn't ask the city council to pass a resolution. I didn't even call any of my neighbors.

I just took a hoe and chopped their heads off and killed them dead as doorknobs. Now, I guess you could call it a unilateral action. Or maybe a preemptive strike. I certainly did not give them the "global test."

I took their poisonous heads off because they were a threat to my family and my home. They were a threat to all I hold dear, and isn't that what this war on terror is all about.

Later there was a vote to fund the war and supply needed equipment for our troops. Although both Kerry and Edwards had voted to go to war, they were so scared of Howard Dean that they voted against giving our troops what they needed to win that war.

Think about this for a minute. Because nothing explains this man who wants to be commander in chief

than this sorry performance. I'm talking about Kerry's vote to deny protective armor for our troops in harms way, faraway, and help for their struggling dependents back here at home.

As far as I am concerned that tells you all you need to know about this politician. It was disgraceful—more than disgraceful but not a surprise to anyone familiar with the Kerry record. In his nearly twenty years, Senator Kerry opposed every single major weapons system that won the Cold War and that is now winning the war on terror.

He opposed the B-1 bomber, the B-2, the F-15, and F-14A, the 14-D . . . the Apache helicopter, the Harrier jet, the Patriot missile . . . the Aegis air-defense cruiser, the Strategic Defense Initiative, and the Trident Missile—just to name a few.

Remember the question I asked in New York City about this man who now wants to be the commander of chief of U.S. Armed Forces? U.S. forces armed with what, spitballs?

This man wants to be the leader of the free world. Free for how long?

Why can't he understand that we are fighting a war over there to keep from fighting a war here?

George Bush understands that we need new strategies to meet new threats.

George Bush knows we don't need sixty thousand troops in Germany protecting us from a Communist threat that disappeared fifteen years ago. George Bush knows the way we handled intelligence in the past will no longer work. He will give the right people the right tools to make the right decisions at the right time.

I have been voting for presidents since 1952—more than half a century—and I have never seen a presidential candidate so out of touch with the average American as is John Kerry. There's a huge gap between this candidate and what most American people think.

Remember that great old movie, *The Wizard of Oz*? Remember Judy Garland skipping down the yellow brick road on her way to that land on the far side of the moon and beyond the rain? That's John Kerry.

And skipping merrily along with him—just like in the movie—arm in arm is the scarecrow who needed a brain—Whoopi; the cowardly lion who needed courage—Michael Moore; and the Tin Man who needed a heart—George Soros, the billionaire who wants to legalize drugs.

And just like Judy Garland lived in that dream world and then abruptly woke up in her own bed back in Kansas, so on November 3, John Kerry's dream will be over and he'll wake up in his mansion in Boston, or the Nantucket ocean front, the estate in the Alleghenies, or his chateau in Sun Valley, or any one of the Heinz 57 varieties of opulent living he has at his disposal. And then he can windsurf in those flowered baggy pants to his heart's content.

Let me just give you a few examples of why I say Kerry is on the far side of the moon and so out of touch with most Americans . . .

Americans, by 87 percent to 5 percent, believe we should limit the benefits for able-bodied welfare recipients to two years and require them to do community work, attend school, and participate in a job-training program. Kerry and Edwards are part of that 5 percent who for three years have blocked a Senate bill that would do just that.

Eighty-four percent of Americans say that murderers of pregnant women who also kill the unborn baby should also be prosecuted for killing the baby. It's called Laci's Law. Kerry is one of the 16 percent that says no.

Four out of five Americans say children should be allowed to pray in school. Kerry is part of that one-fifth who says no.

These are a few of the reasons why Democrats also running this year are running from Kerry. From South Carolina to South Dakota, the senatorial candidates won't have anything to do with him. Tom Daschle is even running a TV ad showing him hugging President Bush.

Same thing in Colorado and for Bill Clinton's chief of staff, Erskine Bowles, in North Carolina. They don't want anything to do with their candidate for president.

And church-goers, think about this: When it comes to confirming the president's judicial appointments, Kerry and Edwards's position is that no Catholic, Orthodox Jewish, or fundamentalist Protestant nominee for judge who follows their religious beliefs should be confirmed to serve on the Federal Appeals Court or the Supreme Court.

Not enough people know that. That is such a stunning secular bias that if the American people really knew it, they'd not just vote against them, they'd ride them out of town on a rail.

Kerry voted against a ban on the cruel and hideous procedure known as partial birth abortion. Kerry voted three times against even notifying—not getting consent, but just "notifying" parents of their minor having an abortion.

And how could this man talk about the glory of Old Glory like he did in Boston when he voted three times against the amendment to protect that Star Spangled Banner from being burned by a bunch of yahoos.

It is the voting record that defines a man. I have told you what Kerry's record is on national security. I have told you what Kerry's record is on taxes. I have told you what Kerry's record is on values.

That is his record. As Casey Stengle used to say about records, "You can look it up." A man's record is who he is. His campaign rhetoric is what he wants you to think he is.

Values are important. They define a nation. They define a person.

Talk about a deficit of decency in this country, it was on display in Radio City Music Hall in July. One after another of these "artists" calling the President of the United States a "cheap thug and a killer."

Whoopi Goldberg waving a bottle of wine and squealing vulgar, unprintable things about the president. And then after watching these liberal leftovers from the Super Bowl halftime show rave on, Long John gets up, hugs them, and validates their remarks by saying these artists represent the heart and soul of America.

Not the America I live in. Not the America you live in. Not the America I want my grandchildren to live in.

I've been around politics a long time, and I have watched a lot of candidates "ambitious to be" instead of "ambitious to do," but never have I seen one with the unmitigated gall of so desperately trying to have it both ways.

Oh, I've seen many take both sides of an issue, but never have I seen one who took four and five positions at the same time. He is now on his ninth position on Iraq.

It makes one wonder if Senator Kerry really knows *what* he believes.

His core values—his moral compass—seems to shift on whether he's talking to farmers or rock stars or whether he's in the Midwest or Manhattan. You notice I don't include the South.

He tells people the people in the heartland that he loves hunting and "crawling around on my belly with my trusty 12-gauge shot gun." Trusty 12-gauge? This man does not even believe in the Second Amendment. He has cast fifty votes opposing it. This man with an NRA rating of F and a 100 percent rating from PETA, the most anti-hunting crowd in America.

On another occasion, he told a crowd of farmers that he had a "passion for plowing." I kid you not. That is what he called it, "passion," and he reminisced how he used to just like to sit on a John Deere tractor.

Well, this man who has a "passion for plowing" must not have a passion for planting or a passion for harvesting or a passion for processing because in 1996 he advocated doing away with the Department of Agriculture or, as he put it, at least three-fourths of its functions.

I don't think that was a John Deere tractor he remembers sitting on. A John Deere riding lawn mower would be more like it.

As I said, I first got to know George Bush when we served as governors together. I admire this man.

I am moved by the respect he shows the first lady, his unabashed love for his parents and his daughters, and the fact that he is unashamed of his belief that God is not indifferent to America.

I can identify with someone who has lived that line in "Amazing Grace," "was blind, but now I see," and I like the fact that he's the same man on Saturday night that he is on Sunday morning.

He is not a slick talker, but he is a straight shooter, and where I come from deeds mean a lot more than words.

I've always believed that it's not whose team you're on, it's whose side you're on.

In this election, I'm on George Bush's side because he's on the side of freedom. He's on the side of the America people. He's on the side of my family.

We live in a time when there may be no second chance. We live in a time when there is no margin for error.

May God bless our president, and may God bless America.

Former Attorney General Griffin Bell and Zell Miller welcome President Bush to Georgia.

Chapter 8

A FAITH IN FREEDOM REAFFIRMED

With the election of 2004, America's faith in freedom was reaffirmed. With the reelection of President Bush, America recommitted itself once again to expanding freedom and promoting liberty. Only the 1864 reelection of Abraham Lincoln, the 1944 reelection of Franklin Roosevelt, and the 1980 election of Ronald Reagan rival this victory as milestones in the preservation of our security by the advancement of freedom.

The election validated not only freedom, but also the faith our Founding Fathers placed in average folks to navigate the course of this great nation.

During the 2004 election, the American people were forced to confront the ghosts of Vietnam as we considered the threats in today's world. And in deciding our role, the American people decided that while we may not be perfect, this country is still a force for peace, for progress, and for freedom in the world. And that we should *act for* rather than *retreat from* that reality.

So America rejoined the contest for freedom, manifested in a new form called the Bush Doctrine. And in so doing rejected our

Vietnam-tainted world-view and exorcised those debilitating demons from the past. After all, no good idea can take root without first weeding out the bad.

To be sure, Vietnam holds certain lessons for America, but for far too many in the media, academia, and public leadership, Vietnam had become the only lesson on using military force and directing foreign policy. Vietnam alone defined them, and consequently defined their narrow view of America.

But there have been many other struggles that also define the American struggle for freedom. The waters of Pearl Harbor, the thick forests of the Argonne, the ghastly ovens of Auschwitz, the turbulent air over Germany, and the shores of Normandy all hold lessons for America. So, too, do the beaches of Iwo Jima, the frozen mountain passes of Korea, the western ridges of Gettysburg, the rolling plains of Manassas, the long-manned watchtowers of Central Europe, and so many other consecrated sites where freedom prevailed.

But ever since Vietnam, all those other sacred struggles were overshadowed by the experience of that one struggle. For too many, all were forgotten . . . except Vietnam.

Many of us can remember when this new view arrived. It was the 1972 election when the ideals of FDR's, Truman's, and JFK's Democratic Party were abandoned by the anti-war Democratic Party of George McGovern. From that point on, a post-Vietnam mind-set dominated our party's policies on national defense. Conventional wisdom held that America was the problem. Perhaps the Communists weren't our enemies after all. Perhaps it was just one big red scare and our counterparts in the Kremlin were simply excessive reformers driven by noble ambitions. Perhaps *our* motives and the ambitions of *our* allies should be suspect!

Their illogical logic continued that the primary output of capitalism was poverty and that capitalism, not the Kremlin's lust for power, was the cause of the armed revolts around the world. They preached that military force never solved anything, and if it did, it shouldn't.

It was almost as if they wanted to protect the world *from* America. They opposed our funding of contras in Nicaragua. They opposed our support for El Salvador against Marxists guerillas, and, as a general rule, opposed our support for freedom fighters anywhere in the world.

Their creed was that deep cuts in existing weapons systems would induce the Soviets to the bargaining table. Their catch phrase of the day was MAD—*Mutually Assured Destruction*—and a naïve belief that somehow a weaker military would protect us from the Soviet menace. These post-Vietnam radicals attacked, resisted, and tried to cancel or cut just about every weapons system Ronald Reagan proposed to win the Cold War. The B-1 Bomber, the MX missile, the Pershing, the Abrams tank, the Bradley fighting vehicle, the Trident submarine, the fighters, and the carriers were all condemned as part of an overly zealous and unnecessary military build-up.

And as the Soviets pressed on with their vision of global hegemony, the "Blame America First" crowd proposed a nuclear freeze, a total ban on nuclear testing, more UN funding, unlimited foreign aid, and unending negotiations. A weaker America was the way to a safer world, they professed.

So when the Berlin Wall fell and a half billion people from the Urals to the Baltic, from Siberia to the Crimea, became free, our leftist friends who had been giving America all the blame now refused to give Ronald Reagan and America any of the credit.

The Cold War was the greatest victory for freedom in the history of the world. But those of the post-Vietnam mind-set praised it not. And so America went into the post-Cold War era, still conflicted. Then America suffered the new lessons of freedom found in a grassy field in Pennsylvania, the halls of the Pentagon, and the skyscrapers of lower Manhattan.

Historian David McCullough has called it the worst day in U.S. history—but was it enough to tip the scales back toward reality? Was it enough to show us that the world is a dangerous place, that freedom is fragile, and that America cannot ignore its role as leader of the free world?

But while 9/11 woke up many to the cold hard facts of life, it also stirred the dormant but undiminished ghosts of Vietnam. The same stroke that unleashed the war in Iraq let loose a host of demons from the past. It was as if the question "What is in the best interest of our nation during a time of war?" was never asked.

The depths of this collapse in national unity can only be understood by knowing our past peaks of bipartisan unity during wartime. There are many examples, but my favorite is Wendell Wilkie who ran for president against Franklin Roosevelt in 1940. At the time, Roosevelt was pushing for an unpopular idea, a peacetime draft. Instead of attacking the vulnerable President Roosevelt, fomenting discontent, and feeding a dangerous and myopic isolationism, deeply rooted in this nation, Wendell Wilkie gave critical support to the president. Further, he made it clear that he would rather lose the election than make national security a partisan campaign issue.

Shortly before Wilkie died, he told a friend that if he could write his own epitaph and had to choose between here lies a president or here lies one who contributed to saving freedom, he would prefer the latter.

That unity was not rare. Back then it was the norm. When President Truman needed support to oppose communism with the Marshall Plan, Republican U.S. Senator Arthur Vandenberg, chairman of the Foreign Relations Committee, stepped forward and helped pass it. Two young Navy veterans who were freshmen congressmen by the names of Kennedy and Nixon supported Truman. Republicans supporting wartime Democrats and Democrats supporting wartime Republicans was a predominant theme in the American body politic.

But Vietnam changed all that. Thirty years later, the post-Vietnam theorists were still stuck in the quagmire of Cambodia. And their tactics were the same. They hoped to achieve their victory by pulling down the president from *within* rather than defeating the enemy *abroad.*

This became their victory plan again. They agreed that regime change was needed, but regime change here at home, not abroad. Their battle cry was "the wrong war in the wrong place at the wrong time." In their eyes, the whole process in Iraq was doomed and somehow illegitimate because it was an American process and not an international process. They smeared our allies, saying they were "a coalition of the coerced and the bribed." And then these same critics attacked the president because he did not have more such allies.

Again and again, they came up with ways to blame America. They claimed our liberation of Iraq after decades of the worst kind of cruelty and torture by Saddam Hussein was just part of a sinister oil grab. America, according to the critics, had created a breeding ground for terrorism, and they called the new Iraq government "an American puppet."

Political ambition trumped wartime solidarity, which in turn risked troop morale and fueled the terroristic insurgents. But their irresponsible and unpatriotic charges and actions clamored on. They knew it was terribly wrong not to provide funding for our troops fighting in the field, but when it came time to vote, they opposed the very funding needed to make our efforts successful. This, I am sad to say, was the most gutless and reprehensible vote ever cast in a time of war.

What can possibly explain such behavior from our national leaders? What could cloud their reasoning so? What could cause them, in almost every situation where duty to country was pitted against political ambition, to choose their own narrow, selfish interests? It was the last gasp of the post-Vietnam defeatism playing itself out on the national stage.

Many of those leaders today, I'm sorry to say, have still not altered their world-view. And, knowing them, I doubt they ever will.

Instead, our hope for tomorrow came from the voters of November. As they judged what was going on in Iraq, they too recalled what happen in Vietnam. But they didn't stop there. From the tragedy of 9/11, our people understood what Churchill once called that "awe-inspiring accountability to the future." They realized their country and their president were making decisions that would affect the lives and freedoms not just of our loved ones today, but for generations to come.

And so throughout 2003, they listened to the debates and they weighed America's role in the world. The World War II memorial was dedicated during this time, and the voters gave thanks, remembering the sacrifices of that "greatest generation." They recalled how millions were spared the tyranny of fascism and how yesterday's foes of liberty are now free, prosperous, peaceful democracies with respect for human rights and individual liberty. . .thanks to the efforts of America.

And then, as we all traveled with our dear departed President Ronald Reagan to his final reunion, our voters pondered the hundreds of millions of free people no longer enslaved behind the Iron Curtain because of this good man and America's resolve to win the Cold War. It was Ronald Reagan's dream, but it was America's resolve that made the greatest liberation of mankind the unappreciated miracle it is today.

So as the shrill charges of the post-Vietnam crowd rained down, our voters weighed these events. They wondered: "If America is not a liberator, why are our old enemies today free, prosperous, and independent? If America creates puppets, why are countries we liberated now free to resist and object? If America is the problem with the world, what would the world look like today *without* us?"

Their answer on November 2, in as resounding a manner as a free people can deliver, was to say that America is what is right with the world. They rejected the post-Vietnam assumption that

Eating with troops in Iraq, January 2004.

America is what is wrong with the world. Voters said that any nation that has done so much for the freedom of strangers, that has brought prosperity and peace to hundreds of millions, that is based on institutions of free elections, free press, and self rule—that nation with such characteristics and such a record deserves the benefit of any doubt.

I cannot emphasize enough the importance of this last point. The worst aspects of this post-Vietnam mentality was *their* "doubt," a paralysis of doubt, doubt ingrained in every aspect of America. But when it came to our enemies, they were afforded the benefit from all doubt.

During the debate over Iraq's fate, we witnessed many political leaders and many in the media granting every benefit of the doubt to a mass murdering, neighbor invading, terrorist harboring, dictatorial regime. The plain facts are that Saddam Hussein not only had but used weapons of mass destruction on foreigners and countrymen, filled mass graves with hundreds of thousands, invaded three countries, and dropped missiles on Israel. He repeatedly and constantly violated UN sanctions, gave refuge to the killers of Leon Klinghoffer, and paid families of suicide bombers in Israel. The civilized world could not permit a man like Hussein to continue to reign. The American voter agreed.

By saying no to the wrong ideology at the wrong time, America has dodged a bullet, and a failed dogma is doomed to wither and die on its poisoned vine. The worst belief of America's past half century has been neutered. America now has the opportunity to reinvigorate the best idea of man, which is freedom. And that is the core of the Bush Doctrine. It is simple but effective.

First, America will not hesitate to use force to stop terrorism. We will act, react, block, and prevent terrorism. Terrorism will no longer be considered a social problem, a political statement, or a criminal infraction, but an act of war, met by the force of the free world.

The second part of the Bush Doctrine, which strikes at the core of who we are as a nation, is liberty itself. Simply put, liberty works. It is not free. It costs. But liberty saves more than it costs.

This new understanding begins with an old question asked in the Old World. In Shakespeare's *Henry V*, the Duke of Burgundy, Philip the Good, recounts the losses and sacrifices of a bloody war that drained the heart of the French aristocracy at Agincourt. Then he asks the once eternal but now forgotten question of European leaders:

> You are assembled: and my speech entreats,
> That I may know the let, Why gentle Peace,
> Should not expel these inconveniences,
> And bless us with her former qualities.

In Europe, where war once raged incessantly, cursing generation after generation, the courage and steadfastness of FDR, Churchill, and Truman brought that "gentle peace" for almost sixty years now.

What great change occurred? Liberty—infectious, incurable, and terminal liberty. After World War II, America fought hard to ensure constitutional democracies with individual rights, and free elections would replace those former totalitarian regimes.

Some said that nations like Italy, Germany, and Japan, with their militaristic background and totalitarian past, could never transit to a new world of freedom, individual rights, and the rule of law. But they did. Eventually, they embraced liberty, domestic cooperation, and agreements based on individual rights ingrained at home. As a result, sweet liberty's spirit has translated into international cooperation and respect.

It showed us all that freedom and the rule of law could extinguish the curse of war throughout many parts of the world. And President Bush has decided to build upon this.

No student of history could ever claim freedom is free. It requires struggle, sacrifice, and endurance. The struggle for freedom is as old as time itself. No one has yet captured this truth better than Frederick Douglass did in 1857 in his speech at Canandaigua, New York:

> The whole history of the progress of human liberty shows that all concessions yet made to her august claims, have been born of earnest struggle. . . . If there is no struggle, there is no progress. Those who profess to favor freedom, and yet deprecate agitation, are men who want crops without plowing up the ground, they want rain without thunder and lightning. They want the ocean without the awful roar of its many waters.

Abraham Lincoln added to Frederick Douglass's statement about the cost and benefits of freedom. In his second annual message to Congress, Lincoln stated, "In giving freedom to the slave, we assure freedom for the free . . . honorable alike in what we give and what we preserve. We shall nobly save or meanly lose the last, best hope of earth."

In a region known for enslavement, George W. Bush has infected the Middle East with an incurable dose of freedom, and thus nobly saved that "last, best hope of earth"—free men.

In a 1936 speech in Paris, two years before the Munich crisis, when no one would listen, Winston Churchill warned,

> We must recognize that we have a great treasure to guard (to share). The inheritance in our possessions represents the prolonged achievements of the centuries. There is not one of our simple uncounted rights today for which better men than we have not died on the scaffold or the battlefield. We have not only a great treasure, we have a great cause.

Civilization deserves protection and has earned the benefit of the doubt. We cannot let barbarians use our civility and freedom to destroy civilization and liberty, nor can we let the barbarian sack civilization simply because he knocks gently. This is difficult. Holding the course for freedom is hard. But with all I've learned from study, age, and experience, I believe, with every fiber of my body, that there comes a time when a civilization has to choose between good and evil, between freedom and tyranny.

I retired from the Senate heartened that the America of our forefathers made, once again, the right choice for freedom. And I thank Providence above for the wisdom our founders demonstrated by entrusting the direction of this nation to the common man and woman. From these ordinary folks in 2004, we again saw extraordinary leadership, and for that we can all rejoice.

Chapter 9

BEING CALLED A LIAR

Even before I had left the stage, my critics in the national media were telling audiences that I had my facts all wrong about John Kerry's record on national security. Dick Cheney, they opined, had opposed the very same weapons systems when he was in the House and then later as secretary of defense under George H. W. Bush.

Now, I learned a long time ago that politics can be a contact sport. And while I tend to subscribe to the notion that all is fair in love, war, and politics, I think most of you would certainly agree that a politician's voting record, his or her printed and stated positions, are fair and proper to discuss.

It is, however, critical that those who are reporting the news make some attempt at accuracy. And judging from nearly 95 percent of the national media, the American voters did not get an accurate report when it came to John Kerry's record on national defense. But the media did not like my tone. They did not like my message. So they attempted to destroy the messenger by claiming that my message was a lie. So, inevitably, after the speech the character assassination began.

It was as if they had, in a matter of minutes, made a thorough analysis of Kerry's national defense record and determined that the liberal John Kerry and the conservative vice president, Dick Cheney, were in fact long-lost ideological soul mates, separated only by birth and hair.

Instantaneously, we heard from Wolf Blitzer and Judy Woodruff of CNN, Chris Matthews of MSNBC, Alan Colmes of Fox News, and the fact finders at the *Washington Post* and the *LA Times* that if you took Dick Cheney and substituted him for John Kerry, or vice versa, the defense votes that occurred in the House and Senate and the outcomes of defense spending bills and Pentagon operations would be virtually identical.

They wanted their readers and listeners to believe that when it came to their voting records and positions on national defense, the DNA of Dick Cheney and that of John Kerry were practically indistinguishable. That they were doves from the same feather, hawks from the same roost, soul mates separated only by Kerry's ever-changing and always quixotic positions on national defense.

As silly as this assertion is, the Democrats made it and 95 percent in the media were only too happy to parrot it. Let me start with the *LA Times* which bought the Democrats' official line lock, stock, and barrel: "The Kerry campaign responded by accusing Miller of mischaracterizing the senator's record, pointing out that Cheney also voted to cut funding for some of these weapons programs while serving in Congress. Others were targeted for cutback by Cheney when he was Defense secretary in the first Bush Administration."

USA Today minimized the negative of Kerry's defense votes: "Kerry voted against large Pentagon spending bills that include many weapons three times in his 20-year career. As Defense secretary [Cheney]—who spoke after [Senator] Miller—recommended ending some of the same systems that Miller cited."

CNN's Judy Woodruff immediately took me to task on Kerry's record, looking me in the eye and repeating precisely the Democratic war room's talking points. "John Kerry voted for 16 of 19 defense budgets that came through the Senate while he was in the Senate, and many of those votes you cited, Dick Cheney also voted against."

Her partner, Wolf Blitzer, pounced on it this way: "When the vice president was the secretary of defense, he proposed cutting back on the B-2 bomber, the F-14 Tomcat as well. I covered him at the Pentagon during those years when he was raising serious concerns about those two weapons systems." When I tried to counter with the simple and obvious fact that it wasn't until the Cold War had been won that Cheney advocated such cuts, and that I had the documentation in my hands to prove it, they ignored the facts and continued on with the Democratic Party's fiction.

And then that Citadel of Sanctimony, the home of the Whopper, the *Washington Post*, maintained, "Miller's list was mostly derived from a single Kerry vote against a spending bill in 1991, rather than individual votes against particular systems. This bill was opposed by five Republican senators at the time, and Cheney, who was defense secretary then, was demanding even deeper cuts by Congress."

Later, a *Washington Post* so-called "analysis" maintained, "Kerry did not cast a series of votes against individual weapon systems, as Sen. Zell Miller suggested in a slashing convention speech in New York late Wednesday, but instead Kerry voted against a Pentagon spending package in 1990 as part of deliberations over restructuring and downsizing the military in the post-Cold War period."

Editorial pages began to chime in, like the *Philadelphia Daily News*: "Miller charged that Kerry has voted to strip the armed services of necessary weapons systems when Dick Cheney as defense secretary, proposed many of the cuts and voted for others."

Was all this true? Were there just a handful of votes by Kerry against defense, and were those votes identical to those by Dick Cheney? Did the media have their facts straight about my speech? And even more important, did they really want to have their facts straight, or did they simply accept without verification the talking points from the Kerry campaign?

Let's start at the beginning: I stated that John Kerry "opposed the very weapons systems that won the Cold War and that are now winning the war on terrorism." I then listed the systems that Kerry opposed such as the B-1, the B-2, the F-14A and F-14D Tomcats, the Apache helicopter, the F-15 Eagle, the Patriot missile, Aegis cruiser, the SDI, and the Trident missile.

Did Kerry oppose the weapons systems that won the Cold War? Yes. Here are the cold hard facts. In 1984 John Kerry ran for the Senate, promising to reverse "the biggest defense buildup since WWII," a buildup he claimed to be "wasteful," "useless," and "dangerous." In one key 1984 campaign document, Kerry identified sixteen weapon systems he wanted to "cancel." All of those weapons systems that I stated Kerry opposed were contained within his 1984 campaign literature except for two, the Trident missile and the B-2 bomber. His opposition to those was reported in press interviews in 1984. Any good reporter could have easily verified these basic facts . . . had they wanted to.

I had a copy of Kerry's literature in my hand during the CNN and MSNBC interviews. I even distributed copies to the press. No one in the media ever reported it. They totally ignored it, even though it was vital to any debate about John Kerry's record on national defense. It spelled out *in Kerry's own words* his complete and total opposition to weapons systems that were needed to win the Cold War and the war on terrorism. But it simply did not exist as far as these experienced and respected analysts were concerned.

In his own words, John Kerry said he wanted to "cancel" the MX, the B-1, the ASAT, SDI, the Apache helicopter, the Patriot, the Aegis cruiser, the Harrier, the Tomcat, the Eagle, the Phoenix, the Sparrow, and many other weapons systems.

Now, if you are like most people, you might examine Senator Kerry's record and reasonably conclude that he opposed all these weapons systems. But not only did the media refuse to make that assumption, they also refused to give the American people a chance to decide for themselves. This, in my opinion, exhibited a profound deficit of decency.

I was told, on more than one occasion, that just because John Kerry said he opposed these weapon systems, it did not mean he actually "opposed" these weapon systems. Go figure.

Especially important to my argument was that this document came out in 1984. This was the very time when America was in a life-and-death struggle with the Soviet Union. The Cold War was anything but cold, and certainly not over. The premier of the Soviet Union was not Gorbachev, but Konstantin Chernenko, an old Brezhnev hard-liner.

This document, outlining John Kerry's vision for our national defense, came out about half a year after the Soviet Union shot down a Korean Air Lines 747 filled with 269 civilians. It came out at a time when Soviet troops were at the halfway point of their armed invasion of Afghanistan; when Cuban troops were in Angola and Kampuchea; and when Marxists insurgents had taken power in Nicaragua and were all pushing northward into El Salvador.

Here, at the height of the Cold War, at a time when we were cutting cards with the devil himself, when our own future, the world's freedom, and the fate of half a billion souls from Poland to Siberia, from the Baltic to Crimea were all in the pot, John Kerry, in effect, said "fold 'em" to what ultimately turned out to be one of the biggest winning hands ever played for freedom.

A legitimate question for an unbiased media to ask John Kerry at the time might have been: "Did you keep your campaign promise of 1984 and vote to cut these weapon systems?" Kerry's answer, which of course was never given because the question was never asked, would have been "Every chance I had!" By 1985, the "series of votes against individual weapon systems" that the *Washington Post* claimed never took place had begun in earnest.

In 1985 alone, fourteen Senate votes occurred on five of the specific weapon systems Kerry pledged to cancel. Thirteen of Kerry's fourteen votes in 1985 were to cut the defense systems he had promised to cancel. He made numerous votes to cut the MX peacekeeper missile, two votes to cut anti-satellite weapons, four votes to cut SDI, then another vote to restrict SDI's use, another vote to cut battleship reactivation, and still another vote against binary weapons.

Kerry's single vote *not* to cut a defense program was on SDI, and it happened this way: After voting three times to cut SDI by as much as $1.5 billion, Kerry finally voted against a cut of $0.16 billion because he said it didn't cut SDI *enough.*

So when it came down to Kerry's record on the weapon systems that won the Cold War, these were the facts; and the facts were totally ignored by Colmes, Matthews, Blitzer, Woodruff, and many others. As a footnote, I might add that there were two other Kerry votes in 1985 to cut overall defense spending, for a total of sixteen votes to dismantle, dissect, and destroy our ability to win the Cold War. And that, gentle reader, is more than a deficit of decency; it is a deficit of duty.

Somehow, the *Washington Post,* with all of its fact checkers and finders, reporters and editors, philanthropists and philistines, was unable to uncover these votes. After they ignored the Kerry campaign's documented position on these weapon systems, they then, somehow, couldn't find the votes in the official record. The highly esteemed, award-winning, investigative machine, that awe-inspiring institution that once produced the likes of Woodward and Bernstein, could find only one vote over a twenty-year career that John Kerry made against defense. That single anti-defense vote by John Kerry was after the Cold War in 1990 or 1991, depending upon which *Washington Post* report you read. They reported it both ways.

Judy Woodruff did better, finding nineteen *total* defense votes over Kerry's twenty years in the Senate, but again, there were sixteen votes in 1985 on defense systems and overall spending alone. She also made the absurd claim that Cheney voted the same way as Kerry on "many of those" nineteen budgets. Yet Cheney and Kerry served simultaneously in Congress for only four of those nineteen annual budget fights.

In 1985, the House in which Cheney was a member had a series of votes on seventeen specific weapon systems. Seventeen of Dick Cheney's seventeen votes were to protect the defense systems: seven ayes on seven votes to protect the MX peacekeeper missile; six ayes on six votes to protect SDI; another vote to protect the Trident Missile; another vote to protect binary weapons; another vote to protect chemical weapons, and another vote to protect ASAT weapons.

During the height of the Cold War, the voting records of Dick Cheney and John Kerry couldn't have been more different. When Cheney repeatedly voted for weapon systems, Kerry repeatedly voted against those same systems. When Cheney supported President Reagan's announced positions in favor of national defense, Kerry countered in opposition. The sole vote of John Kerry against a cut in defense was because he wanted a bigger cut—a cut as much as ten times larger than the one offered on SDI.

So there were differences between Dick Cheney and John Kerry on national defense. It's the difference between the world's greatest military superpower and, well, spitballs.

But Wolf Blitzer took the prize when it came to concocting the best defense of Kerry's thoroughly indefensible positions. Because Secretary Cheney opposed some weapon systems *after* the Cold War, Wolf Blitzer shielded Kerry from his stated opposition to the many weapons systems he opposed *during* the Cold War. He simply dismissed the numerous votes by Kerry against these weapon systems that occurred years *before* and years *after* Cheney was secretary of defense.

According to the Wolf's logic, Secretary Cheney's opposition to two systems in four years absolved Kerry for all his national defense positions for more than twenty years. Blitzer simply granted Kerry a blanket immunity for life against all charges involving his national defense votes and his stated positions.

The main reason I thought this was so important and should be injected into a presidential campaign was that as president, John Kerry would not have had just a vote but would possess a blanket veto. With a veto, his opinion, such as those expressed in his 1984 campaign, would be greater than the combined power of 66 senators and 289 representatives. If ever a man's opinions should be given more weight, it was then during the heat of a hotly contested presidential election.

To their everlasting credit, *Human Events* got it right. A front-page article by Joseph A. D'Agostino, headed "Zell's Right, Kerry's Wrong," laid out in detail the pertinent facts. But hardly anyone else seemed to get it or even cared to check the facts. The difference between Kerry's opposition in 1984 and Cheney's in 1990 was like the difference between opposing the Sherman tank and the B-29 in 1943 and opposing them in 1946, the year after VJ day.

By contrast, Mr. Cheney waited until after we had won the Cold War to propose modernizing our forces and replacing older weapons systems. There's a huge difference. Whether it's the Cold War of yesterday or the war on terror today, Kerry had sought time and time again to weaken our military at the exact moment when we needed to show our strength.

I also charged that John Kerry and his fellow Democratic leaders see America as an occupier, not a liberator. My critics pounced on that one too. Aren't you aware, they sneered, that President Bush has used the term "occupiers"?

In April, the president had said, "As a proud and independent people, Iraqis do not support an indefinite occupation—and neither does America. We're not an imperial power, as nations such as Japan and Germany can attest. We are a liberating power." Are the people of Iraq not liberated from a terrible dictator? Did we not transfer sovereignty over to the Iraqi people exactly when we said we would?

And lastly, my critics loved to point out that I had nice things to say about John Kerry when I introduced him at a Georgia

Democratic dinner in 2001. That's true, and I meant it. But again, timing is everything. I made that introduction in March 2001—six months before terrorists attacked this country. As I have said time and again, 9/11 changed everything. Everything!

I know it's like spitting in the ocean to criticize the media. We all have learned the hard way that the elite media can do and sell anything it wants. We saw the *New York Times* and *Washington Post* repeat on their front pages false allegations made by Ambassador Joe Wilson about Niger uranium and his wife's role in his own activities, but they then buried the correction somewhere in the back pages.

We saw *Newsweek*'s Evan Thomas report that "The media want Kerry to win" and that support, in Thomas's words, "is going to be worth maybe 15 points." We saw CBS News having to admit they were pushing forgeries about President Bush's National Guard service.

The national media's all out defense of John Kerry's indefensible record fell into this same sorry and disgraceful pattern of selling an agenda rather than the facts. What I said in New York was true then. And, sadly, it's still true now.

Chapter 10

CAN YOU HEAR ME NOW?

About five weeks before the election, I appeared again on *Hannity & Colmes* and brazenly predicted the election was "all but over."

"They can see this election going down the drain. I think they're hearing the strains from that Willie Nelson song, 'Turn Out the Lights; the Party's Over.'"

"Do you really...," Sean Hannity attempted to respond.

"We're very, very close to that point now, even though we've got five weeks to go," I continued.

"Do you really believe that?" Hannity asked again. And then Sean turned me over to Alan Colmes. I repeated my prediction: "I think this race is just about over. And I'll tell you why I say this."

Alan then sighed, "Oh, please."

"Wait just a minute," I said. "I've been saying this for some time, and it's become more clear to me as the days go by. No Democrat has ever been elected without carrying four or five Southern states. John Kerry cannot do that. Right now he is behind in every Southern state. In most of those, he's behind in double digits. How does he put it together where he can get the electoral votes?"

Alan answered that he would be glad for me and the Republicans to take the position that "it's all over and sit back."

Well, of course, no one was going to "sit back." There was work to do. The three debates were still to be held and the gap was closing as we rolled into October with all of its surprises.

Going down in the elevator after the interview, Shirley immediately said, "Talk about going out on a limb," and her voice trailed off. Shirley wasn't in the business of sugar-coating. She has always been my closest confidant and fairest critic.

But I was sticking to my guns on this one because it was something I believed down deep in my soul. I had written about it in *A National Party No More*, preached about it to whoever would listen for more than two decades, and now, in the final weeks of the election, I was more convinced than ever that Democrats cannot win without the South. Time and time again this strategy of writing off the South had failed. What made our party leaders believe 2004 would be any different?

Even an old Southern campaign warhorse, the Ragin' Cajun James Carville ignored this historical fact. Less than two weeks before the election, standing in a plush Beverly Hills mansion, James was as cock-sure as I had been earlier: "If we can't win this damn election with a Democratic Party more unified than ever before, with us having raised as much as the Republicans, with 55 percent of the country believing we're heading in the wrong direction, with our candidate having won all three debates, and with our side being more passionate about the outcome than theirs—if we can't win this one, then we can't win s _ _ t. And we need to completely rethink the Democratic Party."

That's what makes a great political consultant. He can tell you exactly what's going to happen and then when it doesn't, he can tell you exactly why it didn't happen. James is a great political consultant, no doubt about that.

Within twenty-four hours of Bush's victory, Carville had completed the autopsy and diagnosed the debilitating disease. Kerry, he said, didn't have a "narrative" but a "litany." I hurried to Webster to understand "litany" better. I found "a prayer consisting of a series of invocations . . . a resonant or repetitive chant of cheering phrases . . . a lengthy recitation or enumeration of familiar complaints." A narrative, of course, is a "story." Then I understood a little better what had happened: *It was the narrative, stupid.*

What he didn't tell us was how the Democratic story can be told or sold with any degree of success in that vast territory between the Hudson River and the state line of California.

I think there are certain inescapable questions about this election that Democrats must answer if they are to be competitive in 2008. And if they can't win in 2008, the Democratic Party is going the way of the whooping crane and the Whig Party by 2020, if not earlier.

Here are the questions I'd like put on the table for discussion:

(1) Why, for the first time since 1920, do more Americans identify themselves as Republicans?

(2) Why did Kerry, the first Catholic nominee since Kennedy in 1960, get fewer Catholic votes than Bush?

(3) Why did the Democrats once again ignore the South and write off one-third of a nation and growing? (Please don't give a dumb answer like "We thought John Edwards would balance the ticket.") *Can they not add well enough to know that if you lose all eleven states of the old Confederacy, it takes 70 percent of everything else to win?*

(4) Why did the Democrats *hire* ground troops, poll workers, and those who work to get out the votes instead of relying on loyal volunteers to do this critically important work?

(5) Why does the Democratic Party insist on letting less than 150,000 of the most liberal Democrats—mostly anti-war secularists in Iowa and New Hampshire—choose our candidate who then has

to go out and try to appeal to more than 55 million voters all around this diverse country to win?

(6) Why did the Democrats give Michael Moore such royal treatment at their National Convention and show up in droves in television's glare and ballyhoo at his movie's premiere?

(7) And lastly, why, in the fifteen elections since World War II, have the Democratic Party's candidates for president only received more than 50 percent of the vote on *two* occasions?

Perhaps when the party's leaders begin to completely rethink the Democratic Party, as Carville suggested pre-mortem, these questions may be discussed. I, for one, would be interested in hearing the answers.

Frankly, John Kerry had several tremendous opportunities to personally change the election, but each time he blew it. Here are three: (1) If Kerry had had the political instinct (or guts) when the Hollywood crowd grew so vulgar, profane, and over the top at the Radio City Music Hall fundraiser to chastise their vulgarity and their lack of sensitivity to the respected office of the president, instead of embracing them and calling them "the Heart and Soul of America," it could have changed votes in a dramatic way. It would have surely said something about the man's strength and character. (2) If Kerry could have resisted that uncalled for cheap shot at the Cheneys in the third debate, it would have helped. (3) If he could have done just about anything for recreation *other than* windsurfing in those baggy, flowered shorts when there was no wind. Even a Democrat like Congressman Charles Rangle flinched at that one. (I'll refrain from saying anything about the Harley hog on Jay Leno.)

And why couldn't this obviously erudite, intelligent man ever articulate a consistent position on Iraq?

The Pander Bears around him should have told him all this, but they were too busy working on more complaints and plans for the "Litany." "I've got a plan for that" became laughable after the first few dozen times Kerry said it.

But so much for the losing candidate—what about the future of the party? Does the election of Howard Dean as the head of the Democratic National Committee sound like a "turn toward the middle" to you? Nothing is going to change. Nothing! I've seen this all before—several times. I know the routine by heart. There will be the wringing of hands and the pointing of fingers. There will be countless meetings, seminars, and forums. There will be new polls and focus groups, but in the end it will be the same crowd doing the same thing in the same way with the same result. The only thing that will change is that it will take more money. Carville, Shrum, Lockhart, Greenburg, McCurry, McAuliffe, Soros, Ickes, NARAL, AFCME—they all have grown a little long-in-the-tooth, fat, complacent, impotent, and very, very rich off the decaying carcass of the Democratic Party. They haven't had a new idea or new way of doing things in years. They are still running the single wing in a T-formation league.

Today's national Democratic Party needs a forced march to reality. But there are no drill instructors or generals who have the "gravitas" to do it, and there are not enough troops willing to make the long march to reality. It's too easy, too comfortable and too lucrative to just keep sucking up to the status quo. Drink a latte, catch a wave, and blame it on the "dumb people" just as London's *Daily Mirror* did on the front page the day after the election. The headline read "How can 59,054,087 people be so dumb?" Or bask in the elitist glow of opinion makers like Gary Wills, Thomas Friedman, Maureen Dowd, and Chris Matthews who claimed they could not believe how many "intolerant" and "ignorant" Americans were out there. But we shouldn't be surprised—the Josephus Chardonnay crowd long ago usurped the reins of the Democratic Party from Joe Six-pack.

Another huge mistake some Democrats make over and over is this class warfare rhetoric. Senator John Edwards built his entire campaign around it. All I can figure is that they once read *All the King's Men* or saw Broderick Crawford playing Willie Stark in the movie and somehow came to the conclusion that this is the way to campaign among the "have-nots." The rhetoric is supposed to resonate with folks like I grew up with, but it doesn't. Most of us find it demeaning. It seems they are saying to us: *You don't have enough sense and/or ambition to make a go in this changing world of opportunity.* Of course, the goal of these "class warfare warriors" is to reach 51percent by lumping all the "takers" in the country together and to hell with the producers.

After my mother took us to Atlanta and got a job working at the Bell Bomber Plant in Marietta, we lived in a tiny upstairs apartment where five families shared one bathroom. On Sunday afternoons, my mother would take her two children on a "Sunday adventure." We'd ride the streetcar to the end of the line then turn the seats around and ride back. It cost about thirty cents for all of us. Our favorite was to ride out to Emory University, through the upscale Druid Hills area with its lush dogwoods in the spring and a beautiful park designed by Fredrick Olmstead. We would look at the stately homes of those fortunate ones who were at the top of the income bracket. I did not realize it at the time, but my mother was teaching us an important lesson. She would point out their beautiful architecture and manicured lawns and would say to us, "Work hard, save your money, and you can have a house like that."

Looking back, I find it very significant that she said "work hard." She never said, "We're not as good as they are." She never said, "Those people don't pay enough taxes." It was an example of what one can be in America if one is willing to work hard and pay the price. There was no envy, only admiration and a yearning to be successful.

Sadly, you can't fix a problem (and believe me, the Democratic Party has one) until you understand the problem. The so-called leaders of the party do not understand the problem, and neither does the mainstream media. How can the party reassimilate into the mainstream of America when its leaders look down their noses at the very mainstream it's trying to attract? I didn't have to wait for exit polls to know that 25 percent of Americans are "value voters." In *A National Party No More*, there is a chapter titled "The Values Gap." In that chapter I make the argument that 25 percent are "value voters" and "always make the difference in a candidate winning or losing." I also wrote that it was "political suicide" to give the slightest hint that one is intolerant of voters' values. My exact words were "There is a big difference between disagreement and disdain."

Where I come from, in the Appalachian Mountains, a "gap" is a low place in a ridge, a pass where one can see what's on the other side of the mountain. "It is a way through," I wrote. No one heard, no one cared, and so in 2004 the "gap" became a wall.

The night before the November 2 election, one hundred thousand prayer meetings took place throughout the nation. Secular elites like Wills and Dowd could not believe that values had replaced pocketbook issues. The next day, the largest army of paid turnout workers in U.S. presidential history went forth on behalf of the Democrats. Not so with the Republicans. The fate of their campaign depended not on paid mercenaries who always prove worthless, but on the strong personal commitment of a grassroots army of value voters.

Bob Herbert of the *New York Times* later wrote that the so-called values issue was overrated. "I think," this deep thinker opined, "a case could be made that ignorance played at least as big a role in the election's outcome as values." Ignorance? Wasn't this the most discussed, televised, and debated election in U.S. history? Excuse me?

Indeed there was another factor, and it's called national security. Nowhere was that more telling than in the number of white women who voted for national security and for the president. In 2000, only 49 percent had voted for him; by 2004, 55 percent went for Bush.

This increase alone was enough to move the popular vote 2.5 percentage points. Another major change worth noting was that 44 percent of the Hispanic vote went for Bush compared to 35 percent in 2000. That increase was enough to move the entire popular vote 1 percentage point and probably came from pro-life voters. There are now 40 million Hispanics out of the 240 million people in the U.S., with 50 percent more in 2004 than in 2000, and still growing. Two Hispanics, by the way, are new U.S. senators—Mel Martinez, a Republican from Florida, and Ken Salazar, a Democrat from Colorado. And remember, another Hispanic, President Bush's nephew, George P. Bush, is waiting in the wings. So stay tuned.

The Democratic Party is now led by Chairman Howard Dean, who says he "hates Republicans" and dismisses abortion as only a "medical procedure." He will work hard, be focused, raise a record amount of small contributions over the Internet, and energetically visit a lot of the red states. My guess is that he will do a better job than many expect—the first two years. There is a mountain of negative research that has been collected on him from "the scream" to outlandish statements stored somewhere in computer and video files waiting to be debuted.

Dean's congressional leaders, San Francisco's Nancy Pelosi and Harry Reid of Nevada (think Las Vegas), will continue to pull the party to the left because this is where Pelosi wants it to go and Reid will be unable to stand up to the liberals in the U.S. Senate like Kennedy, Kerry, and Barbara Boxer. Dr. Kervorkian is not the only person guilty of assisting suicide, you see.

Red state Democrats like Senator Evan Bayh of Indiana, governors Mark Warner of Virginia, Bill Richardson of New Mexico, and Phil Bredesen of Tennessee will be hot commodities for awhile. Pennsylvania governor Ed Rendell will make all the right sounds, but cannot change the appearance of a big city Yankee politico. Should Florida senator Bill Nelson win reelection in 2006, he will immediately become a serious contender. And if his Democratic

Senate colleague wins reelection in New York at the same time, the two could become a pair to be reckoned with.

The dominant figure in the Democratic Party over the next four years is and will continue to be that senator from New York, former first lady Hillary Rodham Clinton. It's really up to her and her gifted but flawed husband just how dominant she will become. Both John Kerry and John Edwards can forget their burning ambition to have another chance; their time in the center ring is gone. They had their chance and blew it. The nomination is Hillary's for the asking, although there are several hazards in her path. The top one is her 2006 U.S. Senate reelection campaign, which could prove to be tricky. Her current political metamorphosis may make her more acceptable to middle America, but it could also make her less acceptable to her liberal New York base. It is a high wire to walk without a balancing pole or a net. My guess is that she can pull it off.

After the last election, Sean Hannity asked me if Hillary could be elected president in 2008. My answer? "The Hillary of 2004 can't, but the Hillary of 2008 might."

I'll never forget a question she once asked me in a Senate elevator after I had said on the Senate floor that "this country is rapidly dividing itself into wimps and warriors." Her question was direct: "Am I a wimp or a warrior?" I did not hesitate. "You're a warrior," I said to a woman I have known, campaigned with, and been in a foxhole or two with for more than a decade. She is one tough customer, untiring and relentless in the pursuit of a goal. She also has the best political strategist in the world at her elbow. If the truth be told, however, he is years behind when it comes to the crucial job of getting out the vote. It's a blind spot for him and his entire old network and inner circle. The victory formula has dramatically changed since 1992 and 1996. It takes more than raising millions, making great TV ads, paying street money, and being sharp in the debates. It has become a ground war of the fiercest kind, and the national Democratic Party has no troops on the field capable of fighting this kind of hand-to-hand combat.

They are Cub Scouts against Special Ops. They don't have the weapons, the warm bodies, or the desire. They don't have the will to go on the forced march it takes, and it will be next to impossible to cultivate that will in four years.

Hillary will position herself much closer to the middle than recent Hillary watchers could ever have imagined. The question is just how far can she go and still be acceptable to them. This will be fascinating to watch.

Just as welfare reform angered but didn't alienate the old Clinton supporters, Hillary will continue her carefully thought out "warrior" image on the Armed Services Committee and add to the makeover with picking the low-hanging fruit of illegal immigration. I also believe she will consider certain popular restrictions on abortion like partial birth, parental notification, even perhaps a waiting period of twenty-four hours with counseling. Ultimately this will have to be adopted by any Democratic candidate who really wants to win. And Hillary does. Senator Clinton can get away with this easier than any major Democrat, even though NARAL and the Planned Parenthood crowd has been the most loyal and militant of her supporters. It would be like Nixon going to China.

For the abortion issue is about to change as the gun issue did years ago. When Democrats saw how much damage the gun control issue had done to Al Gore in 2000, they abandoned it. Remember John Kerry in camouflage with the dead goose? Someone else was carrying the goose, of course. By the way, both governors, Richardson and Warner, have been endorsed by the National Rifle Association in previous campaigns. But so had Howard Dean.

Over the years, the abortion issue for Democrats has become a similar "no-win" issue. More and more Americans now question the shrill, vehement opposition to any change whatsoever. Poll numbers show more and more young voters questioning the old rigid positions on certain restrictions and even the procedure itself.

But even if the minor changes on abortion take place, the liberal flank of the Democratic Party, Washington insiders who carry so much weight in the early primary contests, will be a day late and a dollar short. There is another issue even more divisive and threatening to the party's survival. I'm referring to the question of same sex marriage, which, by the way, was first exposed not by the Republican Party, but courtesy of those nutty, far-out activist judges in Massachusetts and an even nuttier mayor in Nancy Pelosi's hometown of San Francisco who just couldn't seem to get enough of marrying same sex folks on national television.

And this issue is not going to go away for a long, long time. What it will do is alienate the two groups that the Democratic Party can least afford to have divided. The African American and the Hispanic communities, once solid Democratic strongholds, feel stronger about this question than nearly any other. The intensity of the opposition to gay marriage is off the Richter scale, and it's not going to change.

Let me give you an example. African Americans make up 27 percent of my home state of Georgia. I know Georgia's leading African American religious and political leaders very well. I've campaigned with and for black leaders throughout my eight statewide campaigns. In 1974, I was given a plaque by the Reverend Julius Caesar Hope of Macon that stated I was the first white candidate in a statewide race to campaign in African American churches throughout Georgia. I value it highly, as I do the fact that years later when I was governor I appointed the only African American attorney general in the nation and more African American judges than all the other governors of Georgia combined. They are not simply constituents; they have been friends for decades, and it grieved me deeply when Congressman John Lewis, a saint if there ever was one and a friend for more than thirty years, a man I once endorsed and campaigned for over Wyche Fowler in a congressional race, had some rough things to say about my endorsement of President George W. Bush. But to heal the kinds of wounds that only a cherished friend can inflict, I return to the words he wrote about me when I was ending my second term as governor: "An extraordinary man who had the vision and raw courage to do extraordinary things for the people of Georgia and the nation."

But I have digressed. The point I wanted to make is that I know the African American churches and their leaders well. And I can tell you that 75 percent of the African American community oppose same sex marriage, even though their established leaders like Tyrone Brooks, chairman of the Georgia Association of Black Elected Officials; and Reverend Joseph Lowery, longtime leader of the Southern Christian Leadership Council and close associate of the late Dr. Martin Luther King, Jr., see it as a civil rights issue and support it.

In December 2004, Bishop Eddie Long, dynamic leader of the 25,000-member New Birth Missionary Baptist Church in Georgia's DeKalb County, and the Reverend Bernice King, daughter of Dr. Martin Luther King Jr., led a huge march in Atlanta opposing same sex marriage even though it went against the wishes of the old civil rights leaders.

Never again will Democratic candidates automatically receive 90 percent of the African American vote. This key constituency, along with the Hispanic community, is fractured and has become a major nail in the coffin of the once powerful Democratic Party, especially in the South.

I wrote in *A National Party No More*, "The party is no longer a link to most Americans." Each advocacy group has become more important than the sum of the whole. And that is why the Democratic Party is in the shape it is.

But, the Republicans will not win in 2008 without a fight. The Democrats still have one—it may be the last—fight left in them. George W. Bush will not be the candidate and have that loyal band who stuck with him through thick and thin. Those extremely close and clever advisors and those unknown but very dedicated ground troops in the hinterlands, I don't think they can be transferred to any other candidate.

There are many potential presidential candidates in the Republican Party. They range from former New York mayor Rudy Giuliani to John McCain of Arizona, Majority Leader Bill Frist of Tennessee, Chuck Hagel of Nebraska, and George Allen of Virginia. The very able governors Bill Owens of Colorado and Mitt Romney of Massachusetts would have to be included in the short list, as well as the former governor of New Jersey, Christine Todd Whitman. I do not include Governor Jeb Bush of Florida or Vice President Dick Cheney, because I understand both have said they would not run.

And, of course, there is the current rock star of Republican politics, Secretary of State Condoleezza Rice. Conservative, religious, talented in so many ways, she could become even bigger in the Republican lineup than Hillary on the Democratic side.

Nine red states—three in the South (Florida, Virginia, and Arkansas), three in the Midwest (Missouri, Ohio, and Iowa), and three Rocky Mountain states (New Mexico, Nevada, and Colorado)—have potential to be changed with the proper mix of economic concerns and family values. And if many more big pork-laden, deficit-increasing budgets come out of Washington, that won't help. In fact, with the right Democratic candidate and the right circumstances in Washington, it is not too far-fetched to see a Democratic running against Republican fiscal irresponsibility in 2008. That would be a first, but its not impossible. Unless Kennedy, Kerry, Boxer, and their crowd smother them.

But the values voters are the key. I don't see how the Democrats overcome or capture them. They simply will never believe the values voters make up 25 percent of the vote. *Always.* And, by the way, I don't see how any Republican gets the nomination without them either.

AN EXTREME MAKEOVER
FOR WASHINGTON

*Politics is supposed to be the second oldest
profession. I have come to realize that it bears
a very close resemblance to the first.*

— Ronald Reagan (1911–2004)

Decency is dying everywhere, and nowhere is it more
obvious than within the Capitol's beltway. Politicians are
supposed to represent and serve, making your agenda their
agenda. Once upon a time, that's how it worked. Today,
politicians are bathed in influence from lobbyists and special
interest groups. Political parties are on the take. When the
newly elected arrive, they learn to either get in line or go
back home. These chapters look at a deficit of decency and
short-sighted policies that are particular to Washington,
Doesn't Care. These policies and political realities are in
desperate need of a shot in the arm, full of decency. They
remain as, perhaps, the greatest threat to America's vision of
liberty and freedom.

Chapter 11

ELECTED TO SERVE, NOT SWERVE

Noah must have looked more foolish than the town drunk. In the middle of a dustbowl, he spent his days and his good reputation building a boat big enough to carry two of every kind of animal, bird, and reptile. Can you even imagine the ridicule and disdain he must have faced from his neighbors? Imagine how silly and out of touch he looked working toward something that, for all practical purposes, was useless. In fact, he was a joke. A big ha-ha, laughing kind of joke. The man was "crazy." He had "lost his marbles." I know all the adjectives and all the metaphors.

It didn't matter that, up until he began building the ark, Noah was considered an accomplished craftsman who had contributed much to society. All that mattered was that he had embarked on a project that was deemed unpopular, unnecessary, and utterly foolish. Old nitwit Noah had certainly jumped off the deep end. But, you see, none of that mattered to Noah. The patience and fortitude he had must have been staggering. The hope he had in God was surely steadfast. The dread he had for the future must have been nearly paralyzing. Nearly. Because Noah's faith in God, who could make something new, was stronger than his dread. Noah ignored the focus groups, he ignored the favorable/unfavorable numbers, he ignored his party leadership, he ignored the old friends and hangers-on back home. He ignored the rational and popular for the sake of doing what he knew was right. Yes, Noah built a boat that housed animals, but it carried much more than that. When the waters came both down from the sky and up from the ground, Noah's boat carried the future in its bosom.

Sometimes when I think about the future, I get something of that kind of dread. Sometimes I look around our nation and I get worried. Sometimes I would look around the halls of our Capitol and, like Noah, get nervous—almost frantic—for I could see what was coming. Every now and again, the good Lord blesses me with enough sense and stamina to do something good and right. I think about the statewide voluntary pre-kindergarten and the HOPE Scholarship, which has provided college education and technical training for more than a million Georgians. They were programs I started back in the 1990s when I was governor of Georgia. No other state so far has duplicated them, though many have tried. But, for a period, I felt like Noah.

Recently, I did something else that had no chance of being understood and accepted. It was really off the wall. It generated more than a few snickers by the beltway bunch and an obscure, two-paragraph story in some of the papers. My bill to repeal the Seventeenth Amendment was dead on arrival as soon as I introduced it on the floor of the U.S. Senate. In fact, I knew even before I started work on the bill that it had no chance of passing. So why continue? Why not take the advice of the so-called party leaders, pitch in, and support their beloved and generous special interests? Why pull another Noah? I guess I couldn't help myself. I guess, after serving in Washington, I could see how political correctness and special interests had turned too many of our elected officials into purchased puppets appearing on the national stage on behalf of their benefactors and not the voters back home. So I set out to shatter that unbreakable prism of political correctness that had bent the light of truth, allowing elected officials to swerve rather than serve. They swerve to find ways to protect and entrench their own power. They swerve to find ways to reward their big campaign contributors. They swerve away from what will best serve the people back home. Oh, I could see the clouds building and I could hear the thunder clapping.

On April 29, 2004, not unlike nitwit Noah sawing his first plank, I introduced a bill to repeal the Seventeenth Amendment. The Seventeenth Amendment was ratified in the early 1900s, quickly and overwhelmingly. It allowed for the direct election of U.S. senators. Up until then, senators were chosen by the state legislatures as James Madison, Alexander Hamilton, and our Founding Fathers had intended. Those who helped usher in the Seventeenth Amendment couldn't have predicted what a sorry mess we would someday have in Washington. They couldn't have known that one day the president of the most powerful nation on earth would be incapable of appointing judges who received the endorsement of a clear majority of the Senate and the American Bar. They couldn't have known the president would be neutered and rendered incapable of conducting a war without being torn to shreds by partisans with their eyes set, not on the defeat of our enemy but on the defeat of our president.

The U.S. Senate has grown so impotent that an eighteen-wheeler loaded with Viagra would do no good. The House of Representatives, theoretically the closest of all branches of the federal government to the people, is incapable of curbing extravagant spending or limiting our spiraling debt. Incumbents are so entrenched you might as well call off 80 percent of the House races. Is it possible we have abandoned democracy for a coronation of corruption? Since maintaining a career in politics is more important than making good laws, most of the laws of the land, at least the most important and lasting ones, are made not by elected representatives of the people but by unelected, unaccountable legislators in black robes who really make the law and hold their jobs for life.

What this government needs is an extreme makeover, and I am not referring to some minor nose job or a little shot of Botox here and there.

In early 2004, *Congressional Quarterly* devoted an entire issue to the mandate wars, with headlines blaring: "Unfunded Mandates Add to Woes, States Say"; "Localities Get the Bill for Beefed Up Security"; "Transportation Money Comes with Strings"; and "Medicare Stuck in Funding Squabbles." One would think that the much-heralded Unfunded Mandate Reform Act of 1995 never passed. The National Conference of State Legislatures has estimated that in 2005 the total unfunded mandate passed down to the states and then charged to local taxpayers is $33 billion. That's $33 billion, more than twice the entire budget of my home state of Georgia. Make no mistake about it, the current system has put us all under the heel of a distant and unresponsive government, and it gives the enthusiastic tax raisers at the state level who can say "the feds made me do it" the very excuse they are looking for to dig deeper and deeper into the pockets of you, the taxpayer.

It is not a pretty picture. But it's not entirely the fault of our elected officials. For the most part, the folks you send to Washington are smart and decent people. But once they get there and become a member of "the team," they quickly discover that the system is stronger than they are. They discover a decaying foundation to a long since dead republic because that perfect balance our brilliant Founding Fathers put in place in 1787 no longer exists. Perhaps the answer is a return to the original thinking of those wisest of all men and how they intended for this government to function. Federalism, for all practical purposes, has become to this generation of leaders some vague philosophy of the past that is dead, dead, dead. It isn't even on life support. The line on that monitor went flat some time ago.

Direct elections of senators, as great and as good as that sounds, has allowed Washington's special interests to call the shots, whether it is filling judicial vacancies, passing laws, or issuing regulations.

The state governments aided in their own collective suicide by going along with that popular fad at the time. Today it is heresy even to think about changing the system. I know that. But can you imagine those dreadful unfunded mandates being passed on to the states or a homeland security bill being torpedoed by the unions if senators were still chosen by and responsible to the state legislatures whose members are in turn responsible to the people back in their communities whom they know on a first-name basis? Make no mistake about it, today special interest groups and their fundraising power elect and then hold U.S. senators in bondage forever. In the past five election cycles, senators have raised more than $1.5 billion for their election contests, not counting all the soft money spent on their behalf in other ways. Few would believe it, but the daily business of the Senate is actually scheduled around fundraising.

So, as good as it sounds and/or as sacrosanct as it is, the Seventeenth Amendment was the death of the careful balance between state and federal government. As designed by that brilliant and practical group of Founding Fathers, the two governments would be in competition with each other and neither could abuse or run rough-shod over the other. The election of senators by the state legislatures was the linchpin that guaranteed the interests of the respective states would be protected. Today, state governments have to stand in line or put state lobbying offices in Washington because they are just another one of the many special interests that try to get senators to listen to them. And they are at an extreme disadvantage because they have no generous political action committee.

Edward Gibbons wrote of the decline of the Roman Empire: "The fine theory of a republic insensibly vanished." That is exactly what happened in 1913 when the state legislatures, except for Utah and Delaware, rushed pell-mell to ratify the popular Seventeenth Amendment and, by doing so, slashed their own throats and destroyed federalism forever. It was a victory for special-interest tyranny and a blow to the power of state governments that would cripple them forever. The Senate's greatest era of Clay, Webster, and

Calhoun, when members answered to the people back home and not fat checkbooks, is long gone.

Make no mistake about it, the Seventeenth Amendment, along with the Sixteenth Amendment creating the federal income tax, started the growth of big government and destroyed the principles our Founding Fathers worked so hard to create.

Am I naïve enough to think the special interests wouldn't just transfer their money and influence to the state level if the Seventeenth Amendment were repealed? Nope. But I'd bet you it would be much more difficult to peddle influence and buy block votes in a smaller electorate. I seriously doubt NARAL or the Sierra Club or AFSCME would "own" too many legislators in North and South Georgia. Back home, the voters would be watching more closely. To use that favorite of all Washington words, there would be more "transparency." And how!

When I introduced the bill, I said that it "*would* repeal the Seventeenth Amendment." I used "would," not "will," because I knew it didn't stand a snowball's chance in July of even getting a co-sponsor in among that crowd in Washington, Doesn't Care. And I was right. I've seen the clouds. Now I hear the thunder. God help us.

Chapter 12

WITCH HUNTING IN THE U.S. SENATE

"McCarthyism" has been a synonym for character assassination since the early 1950s when Senator Joe McCarthy of Wisconsin defamed good and decent people and ruined careers during his highly publicized hunt for communists.

McCarthy was overly ambitious, played to the crowds, and believed "the end justified the means" as he lied and exaggerated claims against those he castigated as communists. Some called it "witch hunting," and the noted playwright Arthur Miller even wrote a Broadway play that compared it to the Salem, Massachusetts, witch trials in 1692.

It was not one of the U.S. Senate's best moments. But McCarthy's lust for power, regardless of who or what he trampled in the process, is by no means unique in these hallowed Senate halls. For the past two years, a similar and equally methodical campaign of character assassination has been at work. This time the target has been President George W. Bush's nominees to the federal judiciary. Many of America's best and brightest legal minds have had their character and careers impugned all because they believe a judge should interpret the law and not make it. The Daschle Democrats engaged in character assassination of the worst kind and, like McCarthy, they too believe that the end justified the means. Just as McCarthy set his sights on all suspected communists, the Democrats targeted "strict constructionists." They did not want anyone confirmed who might harbor pro-life beliefs and become a threat to *Roe v. Wade*, which is probably within a vote or two of being overturned. The Senate's new minority leader, Harry Reid, a Mormon who is pro-life, has an excellent opportunity to put an end to one of the most disgraceful periods in recent U.S. Senate history.

McCarthy feared communists. Most of the Senate Democratic leadership, like Kennedy and Durbin, fears pro-lifers. McCarthy also knew that attacking communists was good politics. The Democratic members of the judiciary committee know their opposition to these nominees plays well with the liberal special interest groups upon whom they rely for money and manpower in their campaigns. So, just as Joe McCarthy did some fifty years earlier, the Daschle Democrats exploited a volatile situation and hurt innocent people in the process.

After watching the U.S. Senate reject a list of judicial nominees President George W. Bush had sent for confirmation, I stood by my desk with a blown up 3-x-5-foot copy of the U.S. Constitution and a big magnifying glass in my hand, and I addressed my Senate colleagues.

> Mr. President, I stand here proudly next to a copy of the U.S. Constitution. It is a document that has stood the test of time. It is a document that is revered throughout the world. As a history professor, I have read it many times. But I need to know tonight where in the U.S. Constitution does it say the president's nominees for the judiciary must have a supermajority to be confirmed? Where does it say that? I have searched high and low for that clause and that provision. I cannot find it. Maybe

these old seventy-one-year-old eyes are getting kind of dim. Perhaps I need a magnifying glass. [I then pulled one out.]

I seek. I search. I hunt in vain. For is it not there. Even if I had the eye of an eagle I could not find it because it is simply not there. No, the U.S. Constitution says only the Senate is to "advise and consent" on the president's nominees. Somehow that has been twisted and perverted into this unmitigated mess we have today where 59 votes out of 100 cannot pass anything because 41 votes out of 100 can defeat anything.

Explain that to Joe Six-pack in the Wal-Mart parking lot. Explain that to James Madison, that great man who wrote the Constitution. He predicted and he feared someday someone would try to finagle this system, that they would plot and conspire and pervert the process in just the way they have. And he warned about this in Federalist Paper 58. He said if that should happen, "The fundamental principle of free government would be reversed. It would be no longer the majority that would rule. The power would be transferred to the minority."

My words, of course, fell on deaf ears. But I wasn't the first to question or express concern for a system that had subverted the U.S. Constitution.

On June 1, 1950, Margaret Chase Smith, a brave woman who was then the senator from the state of Maine, gave one of the most courageous speeches ever on the floor of the Senate. It has been called the "Declaration of Conscience" speech. Senator Smith questioned what was happening at that time in the Senate. It was not about filibusters, but, make no mistake, it *was* about character assassination.

Let me give you a few excerpts from Senator Smith:

The United States Senate has long enjoyed worldwide respect as the greatest deliberative body in the world. But recently that deliberative character has too often been debased to the level of a forum of hate and character assassination sheltered by the shield of congressional immunity. . .It is strange that we can verbally attack anyone without restraint and with full protection, and yet we hold ourselves above the same type of criticism here on the Senate floor. Surely, the United States Senate is big enough to take self-criticism and self-appraisal. Surely we should be able to take the same kind of character attacks we dish out to others. . .I think it is high time we remembered that we have sworn to uphold and defend the Constitution. I think it is high time that we remembered that the Constitution, as amended, speaks not only of the freedom of speech but also of trial by jury instead of trial by accusation.

Thomas Sowell, in his book *The Quest for Cosmic Justice* (Free Press, 2002), also makes a few thoughtful comments about the role of a judge:

The traditional conception of the role of judges was expressed thousands of years ago by Aristotle, who said that a judge should "be allowed to decide as few things as possible." His discretion should be limited to "such points as the lawgiver has not already defined for him." This view was strongly expressed in a small episode in the life of Justice Oliver Wendell Holmes. After having lunch one day with Judge Learned Hand, Holmes entered his carriage to be driven away. As he left, Judge Hand's parting salute was: "Do justice, sir, do justice." Holmes ordered the carriage stopped. "That is not my job," Holmes replied to Judge Hand. "It is my job to apply the law." Elsewhere Holmes wrote that his primary responsibility as a judge was "to see that the game is played according to the rules whether I like them or not."

Lastly, I want to quote a Georgian named Phil Kent. In his book *The Dark Side of Liberalism* (Harbor House, 2003), he sums up the liberals' view of judicial restraint this way:

> The United States [according to the liberals, according to the Democrats in this debate we are in today] comprises diverse people and cultures. As such, judges should have the power to change laws when circumstances dictate. The U.S. Constitution is a document in flux, and is many times irrelevant in modern society. Therefore, federal judges should be chosen on the basis of their views or the positions of their issues and should be tested on their ideologies.

Many of my fellow Democrats, unfortunately, subscribe to this view and are even willing to obstruct, amend, or ignore the Constitution in pursuit of this goal. For those Democrats, I offer these words from Mr. Kent:

> We are a nation of laws, not of men. Our government is constitutional, not political. Our highest court is the arbiter of constitutional controversies, and the protector of unalienable rights. As former President Ronald Reagan underscored, "Freedom is indivisible—there is no 's' on the end of it. You can erode freedom, diminish it, but you cannot divide it and choose to keep some freedoms while giving up others."

Allowing the law to be usurped by personal views or ideologies suggests that the courts are merely devices to be used to change policy.

Nowhere has that suggestion been made clearer than in the actions of Democrats in the U.S. Senate. Consider several noble men and women who were unfairly singled out for character assassination. Consider the story of Miguel Estrada who spoke little English when he came to this country as a teenage immigrant from Honduras. Within a few years of his arrival, this immigrant graduated magna cum laude from Columbia College in New York and then from Harvard Law School. He clerked for Justice Anthony Kennedy on the highest court in this land, the U.S. Supreme Court. He continued to soar with a distinguished law career until he showed up in the crosshairs of the Daschle Democrats who decided that this good and honorable man didn't deserve a chance of having his name entered into consideration on the floor of the Senate. It is a shame and a disgrace.

Consider Bill Pryor, a devout Catholic and a Southerner who grew up in a house where both John F. Kennedy and Ronald Reagan were revered. He graduated magna cum laude from Northeast Louisiana University and Tulane University Law School. He also has had a distinguished law career, including winning statewide election twice as Alabama's attorney general. Yet the Daschle Democrats would not give him an up-or-down vote on the floor of the Senate.

Then there is Charles Pickering, another Southerner, a grandfather, a courageous and a deeply religious man. He graduated at the top of his law school class at the University of Mississippi, served in elective office for twelve years, practiced law for thirty years, and has served this country ably on the U.S. District Court since 1990. Yet the Democrats in this Senate refuse to give Judge Pickering an up-or-down vote.

There is Priscilla Owen, who grew up on a farm in rural Texas and later rose to win election to the Supreme Court of Texas. Along the way she graduated in the top of her class at Baylor University Law School and practiced law for seventeen years. In her successful reelection bid to the State Supreme Court in 2000, every major newspaper in Texas endorsed her. Yet in this Senate, this woman cannot get an up-or-down vote.

Finally, there is Janice Rogers Brown. I have spent time with this woman. I have read dozens of her speeches. I respect and admire her. The daughter of an Alabama sharecropper who rose to serve on the California Supreme Court, she attended segregated schools until she was in high school and decided to become a lawyer after seeing African American attorneys in the civil rights movement praised for their courage. In 1998, 76 percent of Californians voted to retain Justice Brown, an approval rating most of us can only dream of. Yet this African American woman was not given an up-or-down vote because the Democrats refused to let her have one. I told the Senate, "They are standing in the doorway and they have a sign: Conservative African-American women need not apply, and if you have the temerity to do so, your reputation will be shattered and your dignity will be shredded."

These are the faces of America, men and women who pulled themselves up by their own bootstraps, who worked hard, who played by the rules, and excelled in the field of law. And after all of their hard work and success, they stand in the doorway of the U.S. Senate, one step away from achieving a great accomplishment, and the door is cruelly slammed in their faces.

The result is that today our courts are dominated by unelected liberal activists who continue to make laws, rather than the representatives who are elected to do so. Could it be that we are living in a judgeocracy rather than a democracy?

Consider the possibility that today we are governed by unelected judges who are appointed for life; judges who cite academics and psychologists with too little attention paid to the U.S. Constitution, existing laws, and referendums. There are many examples of how these advocate judges ignore all precedent or case law to make their arbitrary rulings, affecting the lives of all our citizens in a profound and lasting way. For instance, there was not a single precedent cited when school prayer was struck down in 1962.

How did we get this way? Some say it started with the Seventeenth Amendment, which destroyed the original definition of a republic and revoked states rights. Others point to the gradual but certain invalidity of the Tenth Amendment. One thing is for certain, however, the Democracy intended by our forefathers is gone with the wind, replaced by an impenetrable wall, built and maintained by special interests, and strategically placed between elected officials and the people they supposedly represent.

Certainly none of this was intended or even imagined by our Founding Fathers. They made it abundantly clear they wanted the judiciary to be the weakest, not the most dominant of the three branches of government. The sad fact is that the judiciary of this country has swallowed state and local government, the White House, and both houses of Congress. It belched a time or two but then just kept on chewing, incapable of satisfying its insatiable appetite. No mom and pop operation is too small, and no mega corporation is too large. It has prevented clearly guilty murderers convicted of the most heinous, sordid acts imaginable from being put to death because capital punishment was ruled "cruel and unusual." At the same time, this power hungry judiciary approved a process that has taken the lives of more than 42 million innocent unborn babies in the cruelest procedure imaginable.

I am not a constitutional lawyer. I'm not even a lawyer. I'm a historian. And history tells us that when Chief Justice John Marshall allowed for "judicial review" in *Marbury v. Madison* in 1803, Thomas Jefferson had nothing short of a hissy-fit. Chief Justice Marshall continued writing decisions that strengthened judicial review until finally President Andrew Jackson had had enough. Jackson said it all when he responded to a Marshall opinion this way: "Marshall's made his ruling, now let him enforce it." Perhaps what this country needs is another "Old Hickory" to point out what has long since been forgotten or ignored: the chief executive and legislative branch have the final word—if they would only use it.

Everyone today seems to think that the U.S. Constitution explicitly provides for separation of church and state. You can ask any ten people if that's not so, and most of them will say, "Well, sure." And some will point out: "It's in the First Amendment."

Wrong! Read it! It says, "Congress shall make no law respecting an establishment of religion or prohibiting the free exercise thereof." Where is the word "separate"? Where are the words "church" or "state"? They are not there. Never have been. Never intended to be. Read the congressional records during that four-month period in 1789 when the amendment was being framed in Congress. Clearly their intent was to prohibit a single denomination in exclusion of all others, whether it was Anglican or Catholic or some other.

Alexander Hamilton pointed out that "judges should be bound down by strict rules and precedents, which serve to define and point out their duty." Bound down! That is exactly what our Founding Fathers intended to do.

Thomas Jefferson and Alexander Hamilton were often on different sides of an issue. But in this they both agreed. Jefferson put it this way: "On every question of construction carry ourselves back to the time when the Constitution was adopted, recollect the spirit manifested in the debates, and instead of trying what meaning may be squeezed out of the text, or invented against it, conform to the probable one on which it was passed."

Perhaps Jefferson did in fact anticipate these activist judges of recent years. But the sage of Monticello could never have imagined just how much squeezing the Constitution would have to endure. There's no way to put the toothpaste back in the tube, but we can insist that our elected officials seek out judges who will interpret law, not attempt to make it.

The U.S. Senate in 2005 must also change its way or its rules to untie this Gordian Knot that allows 41 sore losers always to win over 59 advocates. What kind of new math is that? 41 beating 59? Yet in the U.S. Senate it is standard operating procedure. Nowhere else in the world, in a democratic form of government, can this occur.

except in the U.S. Senate. On several occasions, as I sought to change this, I asked my colleagues this question: "Is that the kind of democracy we want to hold up as the great American example to emerging democracies around the world? Is that the kind of democratic government we fight for and men die for?"

As far back as May 2003, I joined with Majority Leader Bill Frist to sponsor a bill that proposed a four-step process that keeps 60 votes in the initial cloture vote, but decreases it by three votes with each of the next three cloture attempts until finally, after nearly two weeks, it gets down to the majority of 51. This would give the minority plenty of time to plead its case without blocking the majority forever, as is the case now. I don't see how any fair-minded person can say that's not reasonable.

Chapter 13

A TAX CODE FROM HELL

If our federal tax code is not from hell, its surely from Comedy Central. Either way, its a national disgrace, delivered to us straight from Washington, Doesn't Care. It is a system that taxes those who save and invest their income as much as it does those who spend every dime. I have never understood how anyone could think, as too many of my old Democratic colleagues do, how government can take more than one out of every three dollars earned in this country and somehow believe that doesn't hurt working Americans.

I have never understood how one can think that government taking about three times more of every family budget than was taken at the height of Roosevelt's "New Deal" doesn't hurt working families.

I have often asked when it was exactly that Washington decided the family's budget is secondary, subservient, and inferior to the government's budget. I have always considered a paycheck a treasure to protect, not loot for someone who didn't work for it to steal.

I grew up during the Depression and my widowed mother used to sit at our kitchen table and make more hard decisions in one night than congressmen make in one year. No one could make a dollar go farther than she could because no one worked harder to make a dollar go farther.

That's the secret to the American Dream. And today, at kitchen tables across America, mothers and fathers take pencils to the back of envelopes or tablet paper trying to figure out how they can refinance the mortgage to save fifty bucks a month to help pay for little sister's braces.

At the kitchen table, they decide to fill up the minivan only on Thrifty Tuesdays so as to save five cents per gallon of gas. At this kitchen table, they agree to eat out only on Wednesdays, at restaurants where kids eat free.

On Thursday, they get two shirts cleaned for the price of one. And then on Sunday, after church, they go to the kitchen table with scissors, like my wife has done for years and clip thousands of coupons out of the Sunday paper, each averaging about 75 cents.

Fifty bucks here on housing, five cents per gallon there of gas, then $1.25 per shirt, free kids meals, and a wad of grocery coupons—this is how typical families in America constantly scrimp and save to make their pennies and dimes go further or as my mother used to put it "make ends meet." To make their dreams and those of their children come true, every single penny is scrutinized every single day.

Meanwhile, up in Washington Doesn't Care, the government rounds spending off to the nearest billion of dollars. We routinely waste tens of billions—not in programs but in a single program and not over a period of years but in a single year.

We keep spending going that hasn't been pruned, revisited or even authorized in decades. The federal government spent $24.5 billion in 2003 that we can't account for. We overpaid $20 billion in 2001 and didn't reclaim a dime. We wasted $100 million on unused flight tickets because we never collected refunds on reimbursable tickets. We are owed $7 billion from contractors that we have never collected.

Look, I know families and I know government and I know the difference. Some say that's just the way the federal government is and you can't teach that dog new tricks. That may be true, but I for one am no longer interested in feeding the flea-infested beast. This beast is insatiable and overweight. It grows too fast in good times and even faster in bad times. And once it sinks its teeth into your paycheck, it never lets go.

So for me, I want as much money as possible handled at the kitchen tables of families rather than the cabinet tables or committee dais. Anything that keeps more money at home rather than sending it to Washington is my goal.

They say they want to simplify and reform our tax system. Remember the scene in the movie *Crocodile Dundee* when the New York hood pulls a switchblade knife on Crocodile? Well, you remember, Crocodile looks at the weapon and sarcastically responds, "You call that a knife? Let me show you a knife." And then he reaches behind his back and pulls out a huge blade like a Bowie knife and says to the now wide-eyed punk, "Here's a knife!"

So I say to anyone who will listen, you want tax reform, here's tax reform. We should abolish:

• All individual and corporate income taxes. The payroll tax includes Social Security and Medicare deductions and is the largest tax that 75 percent of the people pay and the most regressive.

• Capital gains taxes

• Self-employment taxes

• Estate taxes

• Gift taxes

• The entire Internal Revenue Service

Abolish them all. How would we run the government, you ask? We could abolish all of the above and, in their place, levy a 23 percent tax to be taken from every one dollar spent on the final sale of *all* goods and services. Such across-the-board taxation would provide the following results:

(1) You would keep 100 percent of your paycheck. Every cent you earned, you get.

(2) It would solve the Social Security and Medicare pending crises, which are enormous with the latter being the greatest challenge. The current dollar 75 year unfunded liability in Social Security and Medicare is $51 trillion. The *total* household wealth in America is less than $44 trillion. If you took *every* asset from *every* American and applied it to our retirement programs, it would cover only 80 percent of the shortfall. And still some insist leave it like it is? No way. This proposal would solve both goals of having a fairer and simpler tax and at the same time deal with Social Security and Medicare. They all should be linked together.

(3) It would also untax the poor, totally and permanently. Each year the U.S. Department of Health and Human Services calculates the cost of buying the necessities – food, shelter, clothing, medical care, etc. This figure represents the poverty level. By rebating the tax in advance each month on poverty level spending, such taxation guarantees that none of these Americans pay any tax on necessities.

(4) It would tax the underground economy which today is guesstimated at a trillion dollars and make every American a voluntary taxpayer.

(5) No agency of government or anyone else would know how much money you make or how you spend and invest it. It would

provide that ultimate privilege for free citizens in a free society, anonymity.

(6) Interest rates would fall, and exports would increase by 26 percent.

(7) The cost of goods would be reduced by 20 to 30 percent.

(8) The Gross Domestic Production (GDP) would increase over 10 percent the first year. It would cost 90 percent less to administer, a savings of $250 billion dollars a year which create the largest economic stimulus package in our history, $2.5 trillion over 10 years.

Too good to be true, you say. I thought that when I first heard about it. This is the essence of what is known as the FairTax. Its daddy is Representative John Linder (R-GA), and the more I waded through the voluminous research my friend, the congressman, sent me, the more I became sold on it. My colleague from Georgia, Senator Saxby Chambliss, and I introduced it in the U.S. Senate in 2004. Congressman Linder has been advocating this throughout the country since 1999, after an extensive and expensive study was completed by a number of scholars from leading universities around the country as well as the Cato and Heritage Foundation think tanks.

Dr. Dale W. Jorgenson, noted Harvard economist and author and co-author of more than 200 articles and books made a final report to Americans for FairTax entitled "The Economic Impact of the National Retail Sales Tax" in 1997 outlining its features and the advantages I have mentioned.

When he compares the FairTax with our current income tax, the difference is dramatic. The current income tax violates the principle of equality. Special rates for special circumstances violate the original Constitution and are unfair. With the FairTax, all taxpayer's pay the same rate and control their liability. The amount of tax paid depends on one's lifestyle and all taxes are rebated on spending up to the poverty level. We all know the current income tax is used by lobbyists and the wealthy for tax breaks and loopholes. It is also used by bureaucrats for social engineering. Under the FairTax, Social Security and Medicare are funded from consumption tax, not your paycheck.

The current income tax taxes savings, labor, investment and productivity not once but many times. The FairTax takes the tax off wages, savings, and investment. It also increases productivity and produces significant economic growth. The current income tax code places unfair tax burden on U.S. imports and fails to neutralize tax advantages for imports. With the FairTax foreign companies are forced to compete on even terms with U.S. companies for the first time in ninety years!

The current income tax code requires massive files, dossiers, credits and collection activity by the IRS. Under the FairTax there is no IRS as the Founding Fathers intended. The current income tax pushes rates up and is biased against savings and investment. The FairTax would increase investments by U.S. citizens and attract foreign investment. The current income tax is an antiquated, unenforceable morass with annual tax returns long enough to circle the planet Earth twenty-eight times. Under the FairTax there are no forms for individuals. Not a single one.

Most people don't realize it but taxes are hidden in the price of everything you purchase, every loaf of bread, every dozen eggs, every quart of milk. They are there, hidden away, "embedded" the economists call it. About 20 percent of the total price of everything for sale in America is a hidden tax. This FairTax would do away with that "embedded" tax and when these hidden taxes are abolished, the price of the goods is lowered and the tax burden is more evenly distributed. This would give us a more even playing field with our foreign competitors and this would mean more American jobs.

Lewis K. Uhler is the president of the National Tax Limitation Committee and an early advisor to Ronald Reagan when he was governor and president. In an eye-opening book written back in 1989, he pointed out that "We pay more for 'being governed' than for food, clothing and shelter combined." He writes "The condition that distinguishes a free man from a slave is dominance over himself and the fruits of his labor." He goes on to put in historical perspective just how the federal income tax amendment exploded the tax burden for the citizens of this country.

He points out that when our nation was founded, the federal government spent about $3 million a year—about $1 per person. By 1910, after 120 years of operation, our federal government spent just over $600 million—about $6.75 per person.

But then came the Sixteenth Amendment which was passed by Congress in 1909 and ratified by the necessary states in 1913. From then on we began to realize that taxation with representation was about as bad as taxation without representation that had brought on the Revolutionary War. Why did Americans support it? The reason was that when the amendment was being debated in the Senate its advocates time and time again maintained that the top amount that would be levied would be 2 or 3 percent of a person's taxable income. That's how it was sold to the Senate and that's how it was sold to the people.

In fact, when one opponent pointed out that if government could levy a two percent tax, it might some day levy a tax of 25 percent or even more, he was ridiculed and laughed at. Surely our elected representatives wouldn't do that to us, they reasoned.

It's impact started out slowly. The law was only sixteen pages. By 1929 the federal government was spending $3 billion per year or about $29 per person. Today the federal government spends $6.35 billion every day or more than $8,000 per person per year. Even after we adjust for inflation, total federal taxes have increased about 6000 percent since adoption of the federal income tax.

And those sixteen pages have multiplied to 982,000 pages and the IRS tax regulations are more than 5,847,000 words. Today, one needs a CPA or tax lawyer just to figure it all out and sometimes these high priced professional can't. In fact, in 1992, *Money Magazine* sent fifty tax professionals the same return to calculate, and not one of them agreed on the same tax liability. To comply with this monstrosity costs the American public approximately $500 billion each year. Think what those thirty million Americans who file a return could do with that. Someone figured out it involved 5.8 billion hours per year, which represents a workforce of over 2,774,000 people. That is more than employment in the auto, the computer, the airline and the steel industry combined. Getting rid of those costs would put about $4–5 trillion in the pockets of consumers who pay these costs over the next ten years.

That's the income tax. The payroll tax is even worse. The poor taxpayer just doesn't realize it because we have become used to its burden. But, next pay day, take a look at that stub and think what it would be like if you could keep that full amount you earned.

It is also regressive, because no one whose annual income is over $90,000 pays the tax beyond that mark. It also discourages hiring because employers pay half of the 12.4 percent.

Also, we currently spend over $38 billion per year on the Earned Income Tax Credit that is intended to refund the payroll tax burden of low-income workers. It is estimated that nearly a third of that is fraud. And the Alternative Minimum Tax, which was directed at the nation's wealthiest, now includes millions of families more than was intended because of inflation each year.

Thomas Jefferson warned, "Were we directed from Washington when to sow and when to reap, we should soon want bread." And yet that is exactly our present situation. New programs on top of new programs on top of new programs are created each session of Congress. With little or no oversight, they're pushed out into the various districts, the congressman puts out a news release, maybe even cuts a ribbon and we go on to the next appropriation/ election cycle and go through the same process, *ad infinitum, ad nauseum.*

Along those lines, I have come to believe that there has been "a poverty industry" created in this country. And in it, the poverty establishment not the poor families themselves, get the real benefit from the multitude of programs which each year expand and grow like "Topsy." The members of this well organized "industry" descend on Washington each year by the thousands—a regular summer blizzard—to visit each and every member of congress, usually more than once. Their expenses are paid from their own budget. This is *your* money, for you see, Congress appropriates your money for them to lobby Congress. They come with their hands out and smiles on their faces, but if not greased, those hands can quickly become fists and those smiles can become snarls in a New York minute.

A not too subtle reminder is always present: their most pitiful is their most promising client. Every group has one. The state staff and Washington lobbyists use them as their poster children to request more and more funding. More, not the same. To keep the budget the same is considered a "cut." Not to increase the program at the percent they request is always interpreted as a "cut." You see, that's the language of Washington: the *same* amount of money is a *cut.* If this sounds like a lament, it is. It is a sad commentary for it is not the need, but effective lobbying and the ever-increasing appetite of the federal government that determines the amount appropriated. That is why we now have the biggest, most expensive federal government in history with little chance of reduction. And that is why I always vote for tax cuts because if the money is not on the Washington table, it can't be gobbled up by this greedy crowd.

And it's all legal just like slavery once was. In fact it is an insidious form of slavery for it requires someone to work for another. That's what our income redistribution practice of today does, isn't it? They are called "benefits" and they make up nearly half our budget. They range from unemployment insurance to welfare, from school lunches to food stamps to Medicare and about one out of

A DEFICIT OF DECENCY

every five of our citizens (not even counting non-citizens) is a recipient of the federal income redistribution scheme.

That wise young French chronicler, Alexis de Tocqueville, who came to America in the 1830s to observe its greatness and predict its future, had the uncanny ability to see that this would happen. In a prophetic chapter in *Democracy in America* called "What Sort of Despotism Democratic Nations Have to Fear," he wrote about this mentality and how it "circumscribes the will within a narrower range and gradually robs a man of all the uses of himself."

He warned that when this kind of philosophy of government dominates:

> The will of man is not shattered, but softened, bent and guided. Such a power does not destroy, but it prevents existence; it does not tyrannize, but it compromises, enervates, extinguishes a people, till each nation is reduced to nothing better than a flock of timid and industrious animals, of which the government is the shepherd.

"A shepherd," I might add, that is very, very expensive and very, very wasteful.

We need a FairTax and a balanced budget where only the amount of revenue growth each year, and not another cent, can be spent for increases in programs. If more money is needed, then cut existing programs to get it. Our tax mess has become a way of national life for so long it goes unnoticed. To continue will deny any buds of decency that consider blooming and will lead to our destruction as we bankrupt ourselves.

Chapter 14

WIMPS AND WARRIORS

By 2004, as the terrible memories of September 11, 2001, began to fade, this country divided itself into two camps: the wimps and the warriors. The wimps were comprised of those who mostly wanted to argue, assess, and appease; the warriors were those who wanted to carry the fight to our enemies and kill them before they killed us.

The wimps wanted to cripple this country in a game of petty partisan politics that was stupid, unpatriotic, and possibly criminal, and cost us in lives and lost time. At a time when the warriors wanted to focus all of our energy on the future instead of the past, the wimps preferred to point fingers, assign blame, and wring hands.

Instead of pouring all our energy into how we can kill these terrorists before they kill us, what did we do? We held a divisive hearing on who was to blame and what could have been done to prevent the planes from going into the World Trade Towers and the Pentagon. Like most, I at first thought it was a good idea; but after watching the first few hearings, I realized we were playing right into the terrorists' hands. Our divisiveness created sufficient distraction, allowing them to regroup and remain a serious threat. There on the big screen we broadcast our worst vulnerabilities for all of the world to see. And while our enemies may not know what great American once said, "a house divided against itself cannot stand," they certainly understood how it was working to their advantage.

What the wimps don't seem to get is that our troops are always listening to this noise coming out of our nation's capitol. And, for them, there can be no 50/50 American support. There is room only for 100 percent Americanism. I was in Iraq in January 2004 and was fortunate to meet with the 1st Armored Division, a unit with a proud history known as Old Ironsides. The issue of troop morale came up, and the commanding general said it was top notch. I turned to the division's sergeant major, the top enlisted man in the division, a big, burly, 6-foot-3, 240-pound African American, and I asked, "That's good, but how do you sustain that kind of morale?" He narrowed his eyes, looked at me, and said without hesitation, "The morale will stay high just as long as these troops know the people back home support us."

Just as long as the people back home support us . . . . What kind of message were these hearings, the outrageously political speeches on the floor of the Senate, and the screaming rants on the Democratic primary campaign trail sending to our troops?

I took the floor of the Senate in an effort to put an end to the acrimony: "Unite America before it is too late!" I told my colleagues. "Put aside these petty partisan differences when it comes to the protection of our people. Argue and argue and argue and debate and debate over all the other things—jobs and education and the deficit and the environment—but please, please do not use the lives of Americans and the security of this country as a cheap-shot political talking point."

The September 11 Commission, with its harsh acrimony played over and over on television, had begun to play a harmful role with the unintended consequence of energizing our enemies and pushing potential allies away.

After listening to all this, I told my colleagues that the commission should issue a report and that it should say simply, "No one did enough in the past. No one did near enough." After that one-line statement was read, I suggested that we then thank everyone for serving, send them home, and get on with the job of protecting this country.

Can you imagine if the U.S. Senate had carried on this way after the attack on Pearl Harbor? Can you imagine Congress, the media, and the public standing for this kind of political gamesmanship and finger pointing after that "day of infamy" back in December 1941? Some partisans did in fact attempt such a ploy back then, but they were soon quieted by the patriots who understood how important it was to get on with the war and take the battle to America's enemies. There are books still being written about what FDR knew when, but at the time our highest priority was to win a war, not an election. That's what made them "The Greatest Generation."

I realized that there were many well-meaning Americans who saw the hearings as "democracy in action," and years ago, when I

Flying with the Georgia Air National Guard in Iraq, January 2004.

was teaching political science, I probably would have had my class watching it live on television and using that very same phrase with them. But there were also the not-so-well-meaning political operatives who saw those hearings as an opportunity to "score cheap points." And there were the Media Meddlers who saw it as "great theater" that could be played out for months on the evening news and on endless talk shows.

Congressional hearings have long been one of Washington's most entertaining pastimes. Joe McCarthy, Watergate, Iran Contra; they all kept us glued to the TV and made for conversation around the water coolers and arguments over a beer at the corner pub. A congressional hearing in Washington, D.C. is the ultimate aphrodisiac for political groupies and partisan punks.

But it wasn't the groupies, punks, and television-sotted American public that I was worried about. This crowd can get excited and divided over just about anything. No, I was concerned about America's enemies who had the blood of our innocent citizens on their hands. When I thought of these evil killers gleefully watching us pointing fingers and playing the blame game, when I thought of them grinning like a mule eating briars and planning more mischief and more deaths, I was, and still am, mad as hell.

Don't think for a second that our enemies don't pick up on the division, the instability, the bickering, the peevishness, and the dissension. We live in a global village where they also watched the president of the United States, in a time of war, get hammered unmercifully. They saw all this and could not help but interpret it as a major weakness.

We should never do anything that will encourage our enemies in this battle between good and evil. Yet, those hearings and the shrill anti-war sentiment expressed in the Democratic Party primary, in my opinion, did just that. In my opinion, we are always playing with fire. The release of Richard Clarke's book, timed to coincide with those hearings, also aided and abetted and aggravated the situation. Long ago, Sir Walter Scott observed that revenge is "the sweetest morsel that ever was cooked in hell." The vindictive Clarke had his revenge, but what kind of hell did he and these ax-to-grind advocates unleash? Only time will tell.

Those hearings, coming on the heels of the election the terrorists influenced in Spain, bolstered and energized our enemies like never before, or at least not since 9/11. That is why I told the Senate in June 2004, "The sooner we stop this endless bickering over the past and join together to prepare for the future, the better off this country will be. There are some things—whether this city believes it or not—that are just more important than political campaigns."

Every administration from Jimmy Carter to George W. Bush bears some of the blame for our unpreparedness. Richard Clarke bears a big heap of this blame. Who, after all, had been in the catbird's seat for more than a decade with more than ample opportunity to do something about the problem? Tragically, it was the decade in which we did the least.

We did nothing after terrorists attacked the World Trade Center in 1993, killing six and injuring more than 1,000 Americans. We did nothing in 1996 when 16 U.S. servicemen were killed in the bombing of the Khobar Towers. When our embassies were attacked in 1998, killing 263 people, our only response was to fire a few missiles on an empty tent. Is it any wonder that after a decade of weak-willed responses to murderous terror, our enemies thought we would never fight back? Richard Clarke should have resigned or been fired back in the 1990s. That is when he should have apologized. That is when he should have written his book. That is, if he really had America's best interest at heart.

Some said "we owe it to the families" to get more information about what led up to 9/11. I can understand that. But no amount of finger pointing can bring those victims back. We now owe it to our future families not to encourage more terrorists, resulting in even more grieving families.

Also in spring 2004 came the unbelievable stupidity of a few American soldiers at Abu Ghraib prison. Again this proved highly divisive. The sadistic sex games and torture pointed out what many of us have long believed, but most are hesitant to talk about because of political correctness. The truth is that there are certain kinds of military missions that male and female soldiers should not serve together.

When the media got this story and the shocking photographs, there was a feeding frenzy. Politicians and talking heads pushed and pulled and shoved and leaped over one another to assign blame and point the finger not at the few individuals involved but at America the Terrible. Once again it was a rush to give aid and comfort to the enemy. And once again I took the floor of the Senate to question this outrage. Here's what I said:

> Of course, I do not condone all the things that went on in that prison, but I for one, Mr. President, refuse to join in this national Act of Contrition over it. Those who are wringing their hands and shouting so loudly for "heads to roll" over this seem to have conveniently overlooked the fact that someone's head *has* rolled —another innocent American brutally murdered by terrorists. Why is it that there's more indignation over a photo of a prisoner with underwear on his head than over the video of a young American with no head at all? Why is it that some in this country still don't get that we are at war? A war against terrorists who are plotting to kill us every day. Terrorists who will murder Americans at any time any place any chance they get.

And yet there we were, America down on its knees in front of our enemy, begging for their forgiveness over the mistreatment of prisoners. Once again we showed the enemy and the world how easily we can get sidetracked, how easily we can turn against ourselves.

Clearly, some of our soldiers went too far with their interrogation tactics and were not properly trained to handle such duty. But the way to deal with this is with swift and sure punishment and immediate and better training. And this has happened. Today the guilty are being punished and more careful screening of who we put in sensitive military situations has been implemented.

But once again, we revealed the terrible chasm between the wimps and the warriors of our country. I have called the former the "Hand-Wringers of America" and warned that if these HWAs continue to bash our country, they will, in effect, hand over more innocent Americans on a silver platter for our enemies to devour. Unfortunately, the election did not quiet them; in fact, some have become even more shrill, vindictive, and wimpier than ever.

Chapter 15

THE UN (THE USELESS NUISANCE)

Nowhere on God's great earth has the deficit of decency become more obvious than that international beacon of bias, the United Nations, whose tentacles reach into every corner of the world. Its army of Lilliputians have not only tied down the great Gulliver, but also stolen his platinum credit card, spit in his face, and killed his children.

It has distorted our laws, perverted our foreign policy, and poisoned our culture. And Washington Doesn't Care; in fact, most everyone is intimidated by its worldwide reputation.

It has many good and well-meaning people working under its auspices, but it is run by a gang of crooks and bureaucratic riff-raff interested primarily in lining their pockets, providing patronage for their friends, and making America look like a villain. It goes its merry way contemptible of American values, American people, and everything that is American. Everything, that is, except American money! The good ol' USA furnishes 22 percent of its budget. It grandstands when quiet diplomacy should be used and sticks its nose into minor disputes better left alone. It has long been ripe for reform, but ripe has now turned to rotten, and it needs to be sent to the trash pile. No one, however, has the guts to drive the garbage truck.

I have not always felt this way. I can remember a time of exuberant optimism. It was 1945. The world's bullies and murderers had been defeated. Our servicemen were coming home. Well, not all of them . . . there were 450,000 who would never come home. But we truly felt we had just won the war to end all wars, and we would not make the same mistake the last generation had made when it refused to join the League of Nations. Over and over, it was said we wouldn't make that mistake again. Most had come to believe the idealistic Woodrow Wilson had been right about the League and his Fourteen Points and that if only we had joined after the first World War, Hitler, Pearl Harbor, and World War II might have been avoided. That's not exactly factual, of course, but that was the conventional wisdom back then.

This time, the thinking was that we would not make that "same mistake" again. The United Nations would help us build "a new world order." We would have an assembly of nations dedicated to maintaining peace around the world. It was to be "the world's best hope for peace." Truly a worthy goal.

So, like most Americans of the time, I fell in love with the idea and the "UN" herself. For this lad, who was already eaten up with politics and noble causes, the UN became my high school beauty queen. I can remember when it was being formed in San Francisco. I knew it had fifty-one original members, and I could tell you that Trygve Lie was its first secretary general. Later I would teach my political science classes about the Security Council, the General Assembly, the Economic and Social Council, the Secretariat, and the International Court of Justice. Listing these along with the duties of each became a standard question on my final exam. Along with identifying Dag Hammarskjold or U Thant.

I was in love with her, all right. She had a heart of gold. Too bad she turned out to be the town whore—or world whore in this case.

Over the years, I watched as she failed not only to keep world peace but also to prevent more and more atrocities, more violence and more terror. I watched as membership was given to the block of Soviet puppet states. I listened to the cheering when Mao Tse-tung's communist delegates were welcomed and the Free Chinese were unceremoniously kicked out. As time went on it became more of a forum for the likes of Cuba and Syria to denounce the United States. I watched as the military forces of the United Nations with their baby blue helmets grew larger while the military forces of the United States grew smaller. And I watched its mode of operation. Under the benevolent excuse of humanitarianism, it would move into an area of regional conflict, call in U.S. troops, assign a "specific mission," and then expand that mission and expand our troops when the conflict was not immediately resolved. With, of course, most all of it paid by with the blood of U.S. soldiers and the money of U.S. taxpayers.

When I finally figured out that this "beauty queen" was neither as "pure" nor as beautiful as I had first thought, I began to look at her other indiscretions. I began to look at her real agenda and discovered it was not pro-American in any sense of the word. It was all about establishing a world government that would not have the checks and balances of our constitutional form of government.

I had not paid much attention to Secretary-General Kofi Annan until September 11, 2001. He had appeared to be this nondescript, more or less harmless individual who had made it into that powerful position through the peculiarly dysfunctional machinery of the organization. How wrong I was! Here is a dangerously deceptive individual with a long history of fraternizing with terrorists and America bashers leading the world's best hope for peace.

Our supposed beacon of hope for the free world has praised Fidel Castro's communist regime in Cuba. He enjoys the company of South African President Thabo Mbeki, who, as the former leader of the African National Congress (ANC), is responsible for committing terrible atrocities against anti-communists in Africa, a veritable war criminal. Annan visited Mbeki's country where corruption and crime are rampant and called what he saw "a beacon of light for the entire world."

William Safire, the conservative yet precise *New York Times* columnist, has written: "Never has there been a financial rip off of the magnitude of the UN oil for food scandal." Jed Babbin, a former deputy undersecretary of defense, in his aptly titled book *Inside the Asylum*, calls Annan's leadership of the UN the "most corrupt—at least so far."

In July 2004, when I was briefed in the Senate majority leader's office about the UN, I found that Safire and Babbin were not exaggerating.

In 1995 the UN created a humanitarian program for the Iraqi people, one of the largest such programs in UN history. The UN was to keep a fee of 2.2 percent on 314 billion barrels of oil with 72 percent going for food and humanitarian needs. It turned out to be a complex and elaborate scam, which provided Saddam Hussein himself with billions of dollars to scatter around as he saw fit. The money that was to go to the people was used for kickbacks and bribes. Those responsible may never be caught and brought to justice, but it's not hard to connect the dots—just remember who was in charge when the UN delayed for months the decision on whether to be involved in Iraq. While weapons of mass destruction were being taken to Syria, Iran, and other hiding places, while terrorists from other countries were pouring into Iraq to plan their later insurgency after the official military operations had ceased, the debate droned on and on at a snail's pace. It doesn't take a Sherlock Holmes to figure out who controlled the pace of the debate.

American soldiers died and innocent Iraqis were killed because of this inaction by Annan. And while we're "following the money," keep in mind that it all started with the secretary-general himself and his son, Kojo Annan, who remained on the payroll of a company involved in the Iraq oil-for-food program even as it was subject to several corruption probes. Fifty billion dollars flowed through French banks, and 42 French oil traders getting 165 million barrels of crude at cut-rate prices. Believe it or not, one of those was the French ambassador to the UN himself.

Doesn't it all seem a little clearer now? This man Annan, who once said that "he could do business with Saddam." Could he ever! Charles Duelfer, a former UN weapons inspector, said in a report for the CIA that Saddam and his government made off with $7.5 billion in cash by smuggling oil outside the UN program. According to Reuters, the report also said Saddam picked up schemes associated with the deal. Ten billion dollars to Saddam and who knows how much to Annan's son may help to explain why, the day after Saddam was pulled out of that spider hole in Tikrit, Secretary-General Annan quickly said that the UN was opposed to capital punishment. Shouldn't this be left up to the Iraqi people?

This sorry tale did not begin with Kofi Annan, and it will not end with him either. Annan has claimed he won't resign. He wants to ride the tsunami relief program back to respectability. But even if he does resign, the UN will just continue to be a cash cow for some other third-rate crooks. Undersecretary Babbin has written that to try and change it "would be a fool's errand, because in order to fix the UN, you need the cooperation of the states that are the problem."

Don't take my word for how bad it is. Many Americans who have seen the United Nations close up and served in responsible positions over a period of time have been more critical than I. A good man like former senator John Danforth lasted less than six months as ambassador. Jeanne Kirkpatrick, another UN ambassador who served during the Falklands Islands crisis, complained that it was "impotent" and "amateurish." Twenty years ago, former UN ambassador Daniel P. Moynihan called the general assembly the "Theater of the Absurd." He continued: "We pretend seriousness to an audience that by now understands that it is all pretense."

But it was UPI senior editor, Peter Costa, who in 1982 painted the truest and most colorful description, calling the UN "roundly disrepected and universally ignored." Further, Costa wrote, "after 37 years of negotiating, talking, and resolution passing, world peace remains an unfound chalice buried somewhere under a desert waste of words."

Proponents of the UN make the argument that we must remain loyal to this corrupt cause or risk the wrath of member nations. But we've been suffering their wrath for years. Take for example a large group of nations who receive millions in aid from the U.S. every year. You might think our efforts to help their countries might also help us at the UN. Think again. Egypt gets $2 billion a year from us and votes against us 79 percent of the time. India receives $144 million annually and votes against us 81 percent of the time. There are many other examples of countries which have received many hundreds of millions of dollars from us, but when they get to the UN, they hate us.

In front of the glass tower that is the UN headquarters in Manhattan, there is a most unusual sculpture donated by Luxembourg in 1986. It is a huge replica of a pistol, a handgun with its barrel tied in a knot, not a military weapon but a civilian one. It is the symbol of the goal of the United Nations to disarm all the private citizens in the world, the "non-state actors," as they are called in UN vernacular. Secretary-General Annan has referred to civilians armed with firearms as "weapons of mass destruction in slow motion." American gun owners are their main targets, but in a UN Small Arms Conference, a treaty was discussed that would have given this international body authority over all the domestic gun laws in the world.

Does this sound familiar? Time and time again history has shown that the first step toward tyranny is to disarm the subjects. Under Kofi Annan, the UN has become the most powerful advocate of civilian disarmament in history. I doubt Mr. Annan understands that the right to bear arms is the right that protects all our other rights.

THE UN (THE USELESS NUISANCE)

One of those rights is also the ownership of private property. Here again the UN is in the forefront of the fight to destroy that freedom. In 1992, the UN held its Earth Summit in Rio de Janeiro. It was there that Senator John Kerry met the wealthy Teresa Heinz, which may have been important to his political career but is not as important as the scary program that was adopted called the Convention on Biological Diversity. Along with it came a 1400-page set of instructions called the Global Biodiversity Assessment. Its purpose, they say, is simply to protect our ecosystems, our flora, and our fauna. Sound good so far? There's a little more to it. You see, biodiversity means all weeds and bugs have certain wants and needs just like humans and they should have certain rights also. Wherever the flora and fauna are located on this planet, and no matter who owns these, they also have rights. "Property rights are not absolute and unchanging, but rather a complex, dynamic, and shifting relationship between two or more parties over space and time," the document solemnly proclaims.

Out of this Global Biodiversity Assessment, which at the time President Clinton embraced enthusiastically, has become a program known as the Wildlands Project. It's the brainchild of Dave Foreman who founded Earth First and once stated that its goal was "to grope our way back to October 1492." In other words, this man wants to take us back to the time when Columbus discovered America. He is opposed to all "resource exploiters," which is what he calls farmers, miners, ranchers, loggers, and timber cutters. Anyone with a hoe in his hand! The goal of the Wildlands Project, and I'm not making this up, is to convert half of all the land area in the United States into a huge biodiversity preserve. No people, just flora, fauna, mosquitoes, and worms. Foreman is Karl Marx painted green. The point is that this fruitcake stuff is sponsored, financed, and encouraged by the UN. Back in 1976, at its worldwide Habitat Conference, a statement was put out claiming that private land ownership is "a principle instrument of accumulation and wealth and therefore contributes to social injustice."

But while the United Nations would prefer to eliminate privately owned property, they do want your help, your support, and your tax dollars. For years they have urged that they, like federal, state, and local entities, should be able to tax and get revenue to run their huge, expensive organization. One of their reports in 1999 pointed out that a tax of one U.S. cent on international e-mails could generate billions of dollars a year. Fidel Castro, always a promoter of the UN, suggested in 2000 that a 1 percent tax on foreign-exchange transactions could raise more than a trillion dollars a year. Castro was pitching an idea that had been floated a few years earlier by a Ford Foundation study, "Financing an Effective United Nations." But even before that, in 1962, our own U.S. State Department issued a report titled "A World Effectively Controlled by the UN," in which it stated "enforceable taxing powers" would be needed. Other suggestions to get your money have been to levy new taxes on aviation fuel or fossil fuels containing carbon content.

The UN's goal of expanding world government through global taxation is a scary proposition indeed. After all, there's no way to vote them out of office if we don't like their policies. Take for example a 1994 UN conference in Cairo on population and development during which health care was defined to include abortion. This conference advocated that $7 billion be spent per year to "expand" its population control programs, including support for China's coercive "one-child" policy, which makes any woman who becomes pregnant with her second child subject to arrest and forced to undergo an abortion. The great "humanitarian" Ted Turner, who has given hundreds of millions of dollars to the UN through his United Nations Foundation, is an outspoken advocate of China's program. Anyone who disagrees with the program, according to Ted, is "dumb."

They further seem to believe that children, no matter where they are born or where they live, belong to the UN. You think I exaggerate? Check out the 1989 UN Convention on the Rights of the Child. That convention advocated registering all children with the state and being able to separate children from parents. At the same time, the convention attacked the influence of the home, maintaining that children have a "right to privacy" and should have the freedom to receive ideas of all kinds, regardless of content. I interpret that to mean that the UN would like to guarantee your children the right to listen to any kind of music they want and visit any pornographic chat room they choose, all without parental supervision. For them, government, not families, come first in raising children. The lesbian anthropologist Ruth Benedict wrote a booklet for the UN on raising small children. It is a universal agenda for establishing a secular civilization, and you and I paid 25 percent of the cost.

I have concluded that we ought to just pick up our ball and go home. Perhaps start a new ball game with a new organization. In today's politically charged atmosphere, few leaders, I am afraid, would heed the call. But I do think there has never been a better time, and certainly no better reason to do it than now. Paul Weyrich, Oliver North, and others have proposed an organization of just democracies. That's not a bad idea at all.

This so-called paragon of virtue that wallows in its own self-righteousness has aided and abetted the killing of hundreds of our American soldiers and has stolen billions of dollars from starving people. Never in its long and disappointing history has it sunk so low. Its anti-Americanism seems so obvious. Born with so much hope and so much promise, we can never again take it seriously. It's time for the UN to go.

In March 1945, a month before the United Nations was to be formed in San Francisco, Winston Churchill made his famous Iron Curtain speech in Kansas. He wished the fledgling organization well, for it was a plan he and FDR had worked on for years. They both hoped great things would come of the UN. In the speech, Churchill said he hoped its work would be "fruitful" and not a "sham." Interesting words from this greatest of wordsmiths. But the next words were even more telling from this great student of history. Churchill went on to say he wanted the UN to be "a force for action and not merely a frothing of words." If the old prime minister could only see what has become of his dream, he would be, I am certain, very disappointed. As am I. As are many.

Chapter 16

SEAL OUR BORDERS

We are a nation of immigrants, and proud of it. The Statue of Liberty and Staten Island are known around the world as the glorious gateway to our nation. We trace our roots back to the long and arduous journeys many made in search of freedom, and many others made shackled and chained. We have served as a safe haven and an enslaved hell. The one constant throughout our history, however, is that we are a nation of immigrants.

But what was once a true melting pot of cultures arriving on our doorsteps has morphed into a mono-cultural monstrosity flooding our borders.

They don't speak our language, and many refuse to learn it. Their medical needs are depriving our struggling seniors, our needy children, and our deserving veterans of critical health care dollars. They are overwhelming and sometimes even closing down our hospital emergency rooms. They are the chief reason our schools are overcrowded. They make up almost a fifth of our prison system with each inmate costing our taxpayers more than $22,000 a year. When they get out of prison, four out of five will commit another crime, and although here illegally, only a few of these felons will ever be deported. They can commit the most serious offenses, escape back to Mexico, and never be extradited to stand trial. They are bringing tons of drugs into this country; in one month alone $50 million of marijuana comes through the Tohono O'odham nation in Arizona. Their numbers are so vast that it is easy for terrorists to blend inconspicuously into their midst.

I am not referring to the Americans of Spanish decent who have been good citizens of this country since the 1840s nor to the thousands of Mexican immigrants who have applied to enter our country and waited patiently to do so. No, the "They" I am speaking of are the more than twelve million illegal immigrants, a population large enough to be the sixth largest state in the nation. Only California, Texas, New York, Illinois, and Pennsylvania would be larger.

With their visible and flagrant violations of the law, they lower respect for the law throughout our society. Yet, if you even mention cracking down on illegal immigration in this country, you are instantly branded a racist and an intolerant bigot. And no one in a position of political leadership in this country—Democrat or Republican, executive or legislative branches alike—will touch this issue with a ten-foot pole. And neither will the business community, including the farmers, because illegal immigrants are seen as "cheap labor," with no health benefits required. Of course, savvy politicians with an eye on the future see them as votes that can make the difference in the next election. Hispanics are 14 percent of our population and growing. The African American population for the first time in our history dipped below Hispanics by 1 percent. So this rapidly growing population of illegal immigrants has become the untouchables of our society. It is the most flagrant bipartisan dereliction of duty in the history of this country. There's never been anything quite like it before. Not even close.

This is the part of governing that requires a strong dose of tough love. Personally, my heart goes out to this vast population fleeing Mexico in search of a better life. They are hard workers and are eager to accept jobs that many in this country refuse. But their unfortunate plight is not the point, and sometimes it is up to our leaders to make the tough decisions. The point here is that they have broken our laws and are using the limited resources of this country in a way that harms our citizens and families. We cannot take care of all the poor people in this world at the expense of our own citizens.

Today, we allow one million immigrants a year to enter our country, which is a realistic number for us to absorb.

Our laws are clear and simple. It is against the law for any person to enter the United States without a passport or visa. Period. But these laws are virtually ignored by our government. In fact, often these illegal immigrants are never even asked to produce such documents even if they are arrested.

So here we are, a nation that is unable to adequately provide minimum health care to our own citizens because we are forced to provide health care to a relentless wave of illegal immigrants. The American Hospital Association has reported that in 2003 there was $21 billion in uncompensated health care services. It is estimated that some 43 percent of uninsured workers in this country are illegal aliens. If you do the math, it is clear that this population is costing us at least $9 billion a year in medical expenses. Add to that another $7.4 billion to our K-12 systems. And of course, add in the cost of housing illegal aliens in prison, and you will quickly see one of the reasons why our deficit is spiraling out of control.

Imagine what we could do for our own citizens if not for these expenses. But our elected officials are turning a blind eye and handing this problem to future generations. But it does not have to be. There's help out there. It's just a matter of priorities. For more than fifty years we have had between 37,000 to 55,000 troops standing guard at that 151-mile border between North Korea and South Korea. The current cost is more than $1.3 billion a year and has been even higher in previous years.

Bring some of them home. South Korea is a vibrant, powerful country with an economy that is the fifteenth richest in the world, ahead of Australia. It's high time they started looking after themselves. We've done more than our share. Their presence offers no deterrent to the nuclear threat of North Korea. So let's bring some of these troops home, redeploy them on our 2,000-mile border with Mexico, our 4,000-mile border with Canada, and give those 11,000 overworked U.S. border patrol agents some needed help. Or let them relieve National Guardsmen overseas and free them up to patrol our borders. Either way, we would be utilizing these trained individuals in a different way and different place rather than creating new government jobs.

To give you an idea of the petty but powerful politics involved in doing something about this problem, let me tell you a true story about a fence. It's a silly battle brewing in California along a section of the U.S./Mexican border known as Smuggler's Gulch. This is a battle between the U.S. Border Patrol and some California environmental groups over a fence—that's right, a fence. It's a fence that was supposed to be built along the western edge of the border, but construction has now stopped. This is a battle that serves as one more sorry reminder of why this country remains so vulnerable to another terrorist attack.

Back in 1996, long before September 11, Congress ordered a triple-layer fence to be built along the fourteen mile San Diego border, from Otay Mesa Port of Entry all the way to the Pacific Ocean. The intent was to curb the hordes of illegal aliens sneaking into this country at that section of the border and to protect border agents from having rocks thrown at them from the Mexican side.

Since 9/11, there is another more urgent need for this fence: It could be the one obstacle that stops a terrorist from attacking the nuclear aircraft carriers and submarines based in San Diego, the biggest Navy port on the West Coast.

Some 10 miles of the fence has already been built, and the results are staggering. The Border Patrol's apprehensions at the San Diego border have dropped from 565,000 in 1992 to just over 100,000 in 2002. That's a decline of about 90 percent. That tells me—and it should tell everyone—that the fence is working.

Well, now the Border Patrol wants to finish building the last 3 or 4 miles of the fence, taking it through the aptly named Smuggler's Gulch canyon and ending at the Pacific Ocean. But they can't. They've been stopped dead in their tracks by some muddle-headed environmentalists who are more concerned with protecting soil and endangered birds and rare plants than they are with protecting American lives.

These environmentalists say the fence will erode the soil and harm environmentally sensitive habitats. Never mind that the Border Patrol has spent more than 1,600 hours studying erosion patterns along that border. The Border Patrol is trying to get it right and to be good stewards of the land—even though that is not their job, nor should it be. The Border Patrol's job is to keep aliens from sneaking into this country. Their job is to make this country safer. This fence will help them do that.

This fence will also mean that some of the agents who are now patrolling the San Diego border could be dispatched to other places along our borders where there is no fence and where we desperately need more agents. But do you think any of that matters to these environmental groups? No, they have halted construction of the fence and sent the issue to court in California, where justice often goes to die.

On the day the commission officially halted the completion of the fence, one of its members seemed to speak for all the environmental groups when he said: "National security is important, but it is not relevant to this discussion."

Not relevant to this discussion? The protection of the biggest military port on the West Coast is not relevant to this discussion? The protection of American lives from terrorism is not relevant to this discussion?

This battle in California is eerily reminiscent of the battle that took place on the floor of the Senate in fall 2002. I'll never forget it. It was the battle to create the Department of Homeland Security. In that fight, the unions fought tooth and nail to delay it, saying we should be more concerned about protecting federal workers' rights than about protecting this country from terrorism.

The Department of Homeland Security was eventually created, just as I am sure that the fence in California will eventually be completed. But it is frightening and frustrating that we have to fight these same kinds of battles over and over again.

Don't these selfish special interest groups realize that the terrorists are plotting more attacks right now and that these petty battles over soil erosion instead of safety erosion only help our enemy? Don't they realize that while they drag the Border Patrol to court over a fence, the terrorists are planning how to attack our biggest naval base on the West Coast?

How many September 11ths will it take to convince these greedy groups to get their heads out of the sand—or wherever they've got them—and realize that what is at stake here is not soil erosion or workers' rights. What is at stake are American lives, those living today and those yet unborn.

I wish we could get some help from Mexico itself to deal with this, but that's impossible. Although their Gross Domestic Product is more than $900 billion, and some of the wealthiest families in the world live there, they too are turning a blind eye. Let's face it— Mexico is riddled by corruption. For more than seventy years, the PRI or Industrial Revolutionary Party did every crooked thing in the book and then along came the debonair Vicente Fox, who won in 2000 and was suppose to end it. He hasn't. It's still a way of life. The average Mexican household still pays 7 percent of annual income in bribes to public officials. No one is going to change this country's ingrained way of life. Even when the country's top officials and Mexico City's finance chief were caught on video running up a mini-bar tab of $2,200 on a trip promoting anti-corruption, nothing was done. So don't expect any help south of the border any time soon, or north of the border for that matter.

America has been invaded by a foreign country, and Washington Doesn't Care.

Chapter 17

LET TEACHERS TEACH

Today in this country, because anyone can sue for almost anything, Americans are literally tiptoeing through the tulips, fearful of being blindsided at any minute by a lawsuit.

And nowhere is that fear greater than in our schools. Legal threats undermine the teacher's ability to keep order and discipline in the classroom. Principals can't remove ineffective teachers. Playgrounds are stripped of swings and seesaws and monkey bars. Many schools don't even have recess any more.

At a time when schools *have* to stretch available dollars, lawsuits are threatening to make the job of educating our children even harder. Take for example the case of a Sacramento, California, man who sued five local school districts to stop students from reciting "under God" during the daily Pledge of Allegiance. School officials say there is a good chance they will be diverting even more money from the classroom to pay for the increased insurance rates associated with the new legal fees. And then there was the Michigan student who sued his school so he could keep wearing an anti-war T-shirt—and won. Or the Texas family who claimed "religious and philosophical" objections to school uniforms and won on appeal.

It's time for a whole new approach to public school reform—something other than heaping on more and more laws, regulations, and rules.

There's a study that shows the average school district implements a new reform every three months. Year after year, we pile new rule on top of new rule. When that doesn't work, we throw more money at the problem. And we wonder why American students still rank only in the middle of the international pack?

Less than one third of America's fourth and eighth graders are proficient readers. And that is unchanged from ten years ago. When a job applicant says he has a high school diploma, it means absolutely nothing. Can the graduate read and do math? It's anybody's guess.

I have always believed that education is the key that opens doors in life. Both my parents were teachers, and I followed in their footsteps and have been a teacher myself.

As governor of Georgia, my two proudest accomplishments were both in education. One was creating the nation's only voluntary pre-kindergarten program for all four-year-olds. And the other was creating the HOPE scholarship so that anyone with a B average could go to college on a scholarship funded by the state's lottery.

So I am a big believer in the power of education to change lives. But today, our schools are spending as much time trying to avoid lawsuits as they are educating kids. Our schools are tied up in knots. They're drowning in paperwork. And they're choking on red tape.

If your child has a special need, the court ensures that you receive all the funding in the world. If your child is deemed "gifted," you also qualify for a bunch of special programs. But if your child falls in the vast middle, you get the shaft. Our public schools have the same problem the Democrats have today: after all the special interests have been catered to, Joe Six-pack's kids are left high and dry.

We need a fundamental shift in the way we think about reforming public education. We need to take the focus off all these rules and regulations and put the focus back on teachers and students.

Of course, schools must be accountable. And yes, we have to make sure kids are actually learning. But we also have to give folks some flexibility to use their best judgment in running their schools and teaching our children.

Just for a teacher to take his or her class on a field trip requires digging through a mound of red tape. When we make it difficult for our teachers to teach, our quality educators abandon the public school system. And we don't understand why there is a shortage of teachers in this great nation.

Ten years ago, Al Gore was talking about reinventing government, and I was trying to bring reform to the civil service system in Georgia. As governor, I wanted our state government to be more responsive to its citizens. Philip Howard wrote a book called *The Death of Common Sense*, and he came down to talk to my department heads. He made the fundamental point that humans have to run human enterprises and that governments at all levels have over-regulated themselves and their citizens.

That's exactly what has happened in our schools, and it's time for a whole new approach. It's time to let the humans run the schools again.

Just ask the teachers why more and more of them are opting to send their own children to private schools. Some will tell you that the only reason they are teaching school is so they can afford to send their children to private school. It's like employees who refuse to invest in stock in their own company with matching dollars to boot.

We all remember a teacher who made a difference in our lives. Mine was a lady named Edna Herren, and she influenced my life in profound and wonderful ways that continue to have an impact on me to this day. Teachers are the soul of our educational system. But today, through our misguided efforts to micromanage educational reform, we've taken the soul right out of the classroom.

How can a teacher read a book to a child when she has her nose buried in a rulebook? How can she interest her students in learning when she is busy interpreting unreasonable regulations? How can she grade papers, read essays, and explain compound fractions when she is required to fill out reams of paperwork?

I know this much about teachers: the vast majority would gladly accept tougher standards of accountability in exchange for more freedom and flexibility to teach their students. It's a simple formula that we've somehow lost track of: tell good teachers what's expected of them, give them the freedom to get the job done, and then hold them accountable for the results. Polling shows that the over-whelming majority of teachers agree there are bad teachers, but they don't trust administrators to be fair and make the right decisions. So, as a result, we have created a system that requires a full-fledged criminal trial in order to dismiss one unqualified teacher.

And what about the students? If you ask parents, they will tell you that in many classrooms across America unruly students run rampant, forcing teachers to teach to the lowest common denominator. Teachers cannot even send misbehaving kids out of the room without someone second-guessing their decision. And woe to the teacher who tries to send a student home—be prepared to answer to a bevy of bureaucrats and fill out a stack of useless forms.

And don't think the students don't know it. If a kid can get a court order allowing him to wear an offensive and unpatriotic T-shirt to school, he knows he can get away with just about anything.

So the fear of lawsuits has helped spawn new rules and regulations, which in turn help protect the bad teachers and turn off the good ones. And the same holds true for students.

What happened to the days when teachers were respected by students and parents? What happened to the days when students were expected to behave or face the consequences? When I was a boy, if I got a whipping from my teacher at school, I knew another one would be waiting for me from my mama when I got home. Those days are certainly long gone.

Now, I am not advocating corporal punishment or a return to the quaint old days of the one-room schoolhouse. Many of the education laws we have passed have helped education. On the fiftieth anniversary of *Brown v. Board of Education*, we should be proud of the court's intervention to assure access for all children. We can also be thankful that the law ensures that disabled children can participate and learn and grow to their potential.

But the sheer number and scope of the education laws we have passed do more harm than good. The law is intruding everywhere in our schools, dictating every single action every single day. We have taken the humanity out of our greatest human endeavor: teaching children.

Why is it that we no longer trust our teachers to teach? Why do we no longer inspire the human spirit, encourage good judgment, and allow firm but fair authority to work their magic in our schools?

Before I left the Senate, I introduced legislation to free schools of some of the legal restrictions that are ruining education in this country. The first was the "Fairness in School Discipline Act." It was designed to let schools know exactly what due process the federal law requires when a student is being disciplined.

There has been a lot of growth in this area since the court's *Goss v. Lopez* decision in 1976. That case said, in very simple terms, that for suspensions of up to ten days, due process means letting the student know what he is accused of and giving him a chance to tell his side of the story.

Now, that doesn't sound too onerous. But in New York City, like many other big cities, the regulations explaining how to suspend a student run more than one hundred pages. And students routinely threaten teachers with lawsuits over routine discipline. This legislation would have been a first step to bring back some common sense in this area. Again, letting educators run the schools.

The other piece of legislation was the "Restoring Authority to Schools Act." This bill says that local officials can decide how to run their schools, so long as they are in compliance with federal law.

There are simply too many crazy, complicated consent decrees out there that micromanage educators' day-to-day decisions, even when there's no ongoing violation of federal law. For example, under a 1980s consent decree, the state of Alabama is not allowed to test teachers to determine if they are highly qualified.

Except for issues of race, this legislation would limit federal court control of schools to two years in most cases. And the federal court's control would be limited only to curing the violation of federal law. Again, let the educators run the schools.

Both of these bills would be just a first step toward a whole new approach to school reform. Both of these bills would help loosen some of the red tape that has our schools tied in knots. Both of these bills would let educators have more freedom to run their schools. And I hope someone in Congress will reintroduce these bills or something similar.

Let's stop protecting bad teachers at the expense of the good ones. Let's stop protecting unruly students at the expense of all the good ones. Let's stop micromanaging our schools and get back to the business of educating our students.

Chapter 18

EXCEPT THE LORD BUILD THIS HOUSE

Whenever I read Psalm 127—"Except the LORD build the House, they labor in vain that built it. Except the LORD keep the city, the watchman waketh in vain." I think of the hundreds of students I've had in my classes over the years and the history lesson I've always tried to teach them.

The lesson begins with a powerful and certain statement: From the beginning, God built and kept this country. Our pilgrim forefathers knew that future generations would wonder why they would crowd men women and children aboard a frail little vessel called the *Mayflower* and undertake a dangerous voyage across an uncharted ocean. So they did not mince words; they made their motive abundantly clear: "This voyage was taken for the glory of God and the advancement of the Christian faith." No squishy words here. They spoke plainly and to the point. It became known in history as the Mayflower Compact.

And they lived by it 24/7, as we say today. With a Bible under one arm and a musket under the other, they carved out a civilization from the wilderness "to advance the Christian faith."

We see these strong sentiments manifested 250 years later in the Declaration of Independence. Our leaders had decided they could no longer endure the oppression of Great Britain. They had no rights. They paid taxes but had no representation. So they met that hot summer of 1776 in Philadelphia. And with Thomas Jefferson, John Adams, and Benjamin Franklin leading the way, they drew up a list of grievances against their Mother Country. They started off the great document with these familiar words: "We hold these truths to be self-evident, that all men are created equal, that they are endowed by their *Creator* with certain inalienable rights, that among these are Life, Liberty, and the pursuit of Happiness." There in the first paragraph, the twenty-first word of the document that defines our nation, the name of God is mentioned clearly and unequivocally.

A few paragraphs later, our first U.S. Representatives appeal to the "Supreme Judge of the World" for the strength to fulfill their ambitious goals.

And they conclude, "With a firm reliance in a Divine Providence, we mutually pledge to each other our lives, our Fortunes, and our sacred honor." The Declaration of Independence has been called the birth certificate of this country. And our Creator, mentioned five times, is clearly this country's father.

These were deeply religious men and extremely brave men. They knew that when they signed that document, in the eyes of the king of England, they would instantly become criminals. They could be arrested, thrown into prison, have their land confiscated, or even be put to death. But they did it; and they did it without hesitation. John Hancock wrote his name very large because he said he wanted the king to be able to read it without his glasses. He also urged that it be unanimous, that they all sign it. He said, "We must hang together."

Ben Franklin added, "Yes, for if we don't hang together, we will hang separately."

So, more than 220 years ago, fifty-six men placed their names beneath the declaration and pledged "their lives, their fortunes, and their sacred honor."

And they did pay the price for freedom. They learned, as we have throughout the generations, that freedom is not free. Of the fifty-six original signatories, five were captured and tortured until they died; twelve had their homes looted and occupied by the enemy before they were burned; two had sons killed in the war that followed; one had two sons captured; and nine others died during the war because of hardships. They all served in that first Congress without pay. Many loaned their own money to the war effort and were never reimbursed.

And when the War for Independence, the Revolutionary War, had finally ended and we had won our freedom, the state of our union was poor indeed. Each one of the new states began to go their own way. They were not "united" in any sense of the word. But our leaders instinctively knew that somehow we must come together; we must be united in the truest sense of the word.

They called a meeting. Only about five states showed up. They called another and announced that George Washington, who had been the great military hero of the war, would preside. They thought that might attract the reluctant ones. But still most states would not even send a representative. You see, they didn't trust each other; they were suspicious of each other. The little states were concerned about the big states. The slave states were worried about the non-slave states. The northern states were distrustful of the southern states. In our beginning, we were divided in many ways.

But the wisest of our leaders knew that if we didn't come together, France or Spain or both would invade and would be victorious because we would be too divided and weak to resist.

Finally, most states sent delegations. They came because they were worried about what might happen if they were not there. There was rancor and division. Once, when it looked as if they were going to break up and go home without accomplishing anything, the oldest man there, eighty-one-year-old Ben Franklin of Pennsylvania, who helped draft the Declaration of Independence, stood up.

This old patriot made one of the most important speeches ever. He got up from his seat and faced his friend George Washington, who was presiding. This man, who invented the bifocals that rode low on his nose, didn't make a lot of speeches, but when he did, people listened. Franklin was the "E. F. Hutton" of his time.

He first reminded them that when they had declared independence just a few years earlier, "We were sensible to danger." I love that phrase "sensible to danger." It's a face-saving way of saying *scared to death*. He went on to remind them that, at the time, "We prayed for divine guidance in this very room. Our prayers were heard and graciously answered." The room was so quiet you might've heard a pin drop. He then asked, "Have we forgotten that powerful friend, or do we imagine that we no longer need His assistance?"

They were listening closely now as he continued: "I have lived a long, long time, and the longer I live, the more convincing proof I see of this truth; that God governs the affairs of man. And, if a sparrow cannot fall to the ground without His notice, is it probable that an empire can rise without His assistance?" The answer was clear, but still no one uttered a word. "I now make a motion that we take a break and that we pray for Divine Guidance." They did, and when they returned a few days later, they found a renewed atmosphere of trust and mutual respect allowing them to finish their great work.

It is so clear that God has been at work in this country from the beginning. God-fearing, God-worshiping men were leading it. "Except the Lord built the House, they labor in vain that build it."

Alexis de Tocqueville was a young French journalist who came over in the early 1800s to travel the country and write an assessment of what he found, what made this new country so great. No one had done it before. No one has done it so well since. No one has ever gotten it more right. He wrote the following in his book titled *Democracy in America*:

> In the end, the state of the Union comes down to the character of the people. I sought for the greatness and genius of America in her commodious harbors, her ample rivers, and it was not there. I sought for it in the fertile fields, and boundless prairies, and it was not there. I sought it in her rich mines, and vast world commerce, and it was not there. I sought it in her democratic Congress and her matchless Constitution, and it was not there. Not until I went into the churches of America and heard her pulpits aflame with righteousness did I understand the secret of her genius and power. America is great because she is good, and if America ever ceases to be good, she will cease to be great. The safeguard of morality is religion, and morality is the best security of law as well as the surest pledge of freedom.

Every president from George Washington to George W. Bush has included some reference to God in his inaugural address. Our money is stamped with "In God We Trust." Above the door of the Senate where I once served are the words "In God We Trust." Abraham Lincoln called the Bible the greatest gift God gave to man. In Lincoln's Gettysburg Address, and engraved on the wall at the Lincoln Memorial, are these immortal words: "That this nation under God shall have a new birth of freedom, and that government of the people, by the people, for the people shall not perish from this earth."

But recently an ultraliberal district court sided with an atheist to remove "Under God" from our Pledge of Allegiance. What's next? Will the courts have us sand blasting the name of God from all of our public buildings? Will we be required to purge the name of God from the stately buildings and monuments of our nation's Capitol? What about the Scriptures from Luke and Proverbs etched into the

Washington Memorial? If a child is not allowed to lead his class in prayer, then why should that same class be allowed to visit the Tomb of the Unknown Soldier and read the words "Here lies an American soldier, Known but to God"? And shouldn't the Supreme Court crier, who begins each day of court with these words, "God save this honorable court," be censored? And while we're at it, let's go ahead and sue both Houses of Congress for starting their days with daily prayers and the Pledge of Allegiance. I shudder to make such preposterous proposals because I am afraid to say they may come true.

The World War II Memorial in Washington was long in coming and is a beautiful and fitting monument to all those who served. But how disappointed I was to note that on the Pacific side, President Franklin D. Roosevelt's famous Infamy speech of December 8, 1941, is quoted "With confidence in our armed forces—with the unbounded determination of our people—we will gain the inevitable triumph." The next line—"So help us God"—is not included. How very disappointing.

I believe—and perhaps many of you do too—that the very soul of our nation is at stake. These unelected legislators in black robes have handed down decisions that are calling into question, as de Tocqueville once described, "the secret of (our) genius and power." Today we're being tested not just by the terrorists but by the secularists. But if we know and remember where, and who, we came from, the road to future greatness will grow clearer. We must never forget "Except the Lord build the House, they labor in vain that build it."

NATIONWIDE WOES

Democracy is a device that ensures we shall
be governed no better than we deserve.

— George Bernard Shaw (1856–1950)

Not all the blame for the low water mark of decency in America can be laid at the feet of our politicians. While they do much to our detriment, the voting public ultimately has the power to call them to a higher standard. Unfortunately, decency is dwindling at home, at school, on the playing field, in the shopping malls, and in nearly all our communities. The strength of our union depends on the strength of our collective character and virtue. If this is true, then may God help us. In these chapters, I point to the problems that result from the lack of decency that extends beyond the Beltway and the political process. These are the kinds of problems that face every state, every city, and every family. They are challenges that can be and should be solved by politicians, community leaders, teachers, parents, and churches.

Chapter 19

I HAVE A FEAR

Jeremiah, the Old Testament prophet, couldn't have been elected dogcatcher. Politicians pride themselves with remaining "on message," which means making sure they remember the three important points yielded from the polls that day. The high-priced consultants tell their candidates that if you stick to the message, you've got a better chance at looking impressive and getting reelected.

Jeremiah's political problem wasn't that he was off message. Jeremiah's problem was that he was *on* message. Unfortunately, his message was of pending judgment and doom. "I must shout 'Violence and destruction'" (Jeremiah 20:7).

You must keep in mind how powerful the spoken word was back then. It was God who *spoke* the world into existence. Then Jesus *pronounced* the forgiveness of sins. So, the potential for destruction with one's tongue is a major part of what the Bible teaches us about being a child of God. For a prophet of God, like Jeremiah, saying a thing was as real as the actual thing. To speak a word of doom was as bad as the doom itself.

When something was spoken, it set into motion an irreversible reality. The only thing left was the actual experience of the reality—

for them, a smaller detail. When Jeremiah spoke of pending doom, violence, and destruction, it ripped at his heart just as if he'd seen it firsthand.

Jeremiah would look at us strangely if he heard us teaching our children today that "sticks and stones may break your bones, but words will never harm you." I'm not sure we're doing America any favor by teaching children at such an impressionable age that what they say or what they hear in their songs and movies doesn't matter all that much. God help us.

Jeremiah's message wasn't popular. Jeremiah's message wouldn't win him any leadership positions. Jeremiah's message wouldn't make him hip with the left coast crowd or some of the oracles of higher learning. Jeremiah's message was a burden carried by a broken heart from a weary prophet. But if carrying God's message was a burden, surely for Jeremiah, failure to be the carrier would have been even a greater pain to bear. Listen to him:

> O LORD, you have enticed me, and I was enticed; you have overpowered me, and you have prevailed. I have become a laughingstock all day long; everyone mocks me. For whenever I speak, I must cry out, I must shout, "Violence and destruction!" For the word of the LORD has become for me a reproach and derision all day long. If I say, "I will not mention him, or speak any more in his name," then within me there is something like a burning fire shut up in my bones; I am weary with holding it in, and I cannot. (Jeremiah 20:7-9)

Jeremiah is the perfect picture of the reluctant, years-weary, heartbroken prophet.

Now, I'm neither perfect nor prophetic nor reluctant. But I am heartbroken. Martin Luther King Jr. changed the world with his "I Have a Dream" speech. I'm not going to change the world or, perhaps, even your thinking, but I've got a message burning inside of me called "I Have a Fear." It pains me to no end when I look at the state of today's family, and I fear where we're headed. We can talk about a great America all we want. We can talk about the great system of government we have. We can talk about the checks and balances we have. We can brag about how we can grow an economy, assemble a fighting force the likes of which the world has never known. America is a grand place, but we are eating our own seed corn if we fail to recognize the importance of strong and healthy families.

Without healthy families, a healthy nation doesn't have a chance. It takes healthy families to raise wise children, support strong communities, and pass along the important values of decency and responsibility.

I've got a broken heart when I consider the state of families in today's America. Today's families are stretched too thin and yet, they keep reaching for more. It was once assumed that the technological advances of the middle of this century were going to make America a promised land for the family. In theory, we were supposed to be, by now, working less, enjoying more free time, and becoming more refined. The four-day workweek was expected to become the norm because it simply wasn't supposed to take as long to get the same thing done.

The microwave oven, the personal computer, cell phone, the relative ease of travel from place to place on our interstate system all taken together, we should be living high on the hog. Who could have imagined fifty years ago that with all these improvements to American life we would have such a sorry yield? Unprecedented divorce rates give marriage about a 50/50 shot (this is even holding true among active Christian faithful for whom marriage is a sacred vow); grandparents have to raise discarded children by drug-ridden mothers and unknown or uncaring fathers; everyone knows what the phrase "latchkey children" means and can still sleep at night; personal debt rates make a checkbook bleed; and wannabe stars are so hungry for attention and "success" that they lower themselves to eat what your mama would have swept out of the house on what is becoming a standard of entertainment known as "reality TV." If Jeremiah were to walk our streets, at least he'd know what to say. "Same song, second verse."

Decency is dying in our homes and in our streets. Like the political spin cycle in which we seem to be stuck, it is a self-fulfilling prophecy of sorts.

America was once a nation sustained by what I call primary producers. Everyone produced. Everyone's hands had some blister or callous from making something. It was simply a way of life. A hundred years ago, farming was the norm; even for many of the city dwellers, gardening was important. Chances are you could at least point in the direction of the farm from which your milk was produced. If you ate, it was because you or someone in your family prepared it. Our towns had a restaurant or diner, but nothing like the cloning of eateries we see today. Having supper in a restaurant was once a special event in a given week. Now, children grow up assuming the rare home-cooked meal is what is special.

After being a nation of primary producers, America then became a nation of industrialized producers. The manufacturing economy blossomed, and factories sprang up. The Northern states received the benefit of Southern boys fresh from WWII and the Korean War who headed to Detroit, Chicago, and Indianapolis to work on the assembly lines making everything from jet engines to Pontiacs. "By day they made the cars, by night they made the bars," Mel Tillis wrote in *Detroit City*.

The subdivision was invented, and folks went to live in the suburbs. Televisions became a fixture in every American household. Shopping centers and then mega-malls sprang up. America was a producing machine and learned to consume the good things it produced. By the end of the last century, America had nearly completely molded itself into a nation of consumers.

Walk around your house and look at the things you've bought in the last year. Read the small print about where these things were made. Give yourself a cookie if you can speak the language of the person whose hands put it together. In townships across this land, what was once the downtown center of commerce has now become the land of antique stores and five-dollar cups of coffee—in a cheap paper cup. All the little shops that were once there—men's clothes, the watch shop, children's stores, ladies clothing, shoe stores, the hardware store—have all been swallowed up by some mammoth structure out there on the outskirts of town where land was cheaper and the corn was growing well. And the local government with that awesome power called "eminent domain" can condemn it and take it over with the excuse, "It will improve the tax base." What difference would another 60 acres of pavement make? Again, like with the explosion of the telecommunication industry, there's nothing inherently wrong or bad with growing a retail economy. But there are consequences, and don't think there aren't.

In an earlier chapter I embarrassed myself as an armchair neuroscientist. I'm about to make the same mistake. That being said, it appears to me that America has evolved to the point of making consuming its prime preoccupation. What lesson is there for us that the phrase "shopping therapy" needs no explanation?

The line between family entertainment and going to town to pick up some necessary items has been not only blurred, but obliterated. There are now malls with roller coasters and sixteen movie theaters. In my neighboring state of Tennessee, Opryland amusement park, where thrill rides and great music once could keep a family busy all day, was shut down. In its place now stands Opry Mills, a shopping mall where families keep themselves busy all day, consuming.

What's wrong with being a nation of consumers? Being a nation of consumers teaches us things that, ultimately, will work to our ruin. It takes habits that would have been an oddity in an earlier time and elevates them to normalcy. Keeping up with the latest fashion, finding the perfect color for your cell phone cover, the ladies T-shirt that shows off your belly button so perfectly, and leasing a new car every two years because the eighteen-month-old one you're driving looks out of touch, I ask you, are these habits of reason? Are they wrong? No. But, are they reasonable? As a fellow Georgian I know tells his kids, the answer is in the question.

What's wrong with being a nation of consumers? It feeds a self-fulfilling prophecy that will eventually unravel the national fabric made up of families, that's what! Before you quit reading and call your chamber of commerce to complain about how anti-business I am, hear me out. The Joneses must have found a newly discovered trust fund because keeping up with them takes more shopping and spending now than it once did. I've never taken that "new math," and I don't own a calculator, but I did learn my multiplication tables and it's obvious to me that buying more means spending more, spending more means earning more, earning more means working more, working more means being at home less, being at home less means being with children less, and that means less time helping them with homework, less time for eating meals together, less time for volunteering somewhere together, less time to worship together. That's what my math tells me.

The unnervingly simple truth is that becoming a nation of consumers is taking away our opportunities to do the things that made America what it is. Am I overreacting? Consider these facts. In 2003, 1.6 million American households claimed bankruptcy. According to our Federal Reserve, U.S. personal debt topped one trillion dollars for the first time in 1994. (Can you tell me if one trillion is a million million or a thousand billion?) Sixty percent of households with credit cards carry an average monthly balance of $13,000, which doesn't even include monthly car and house payments. Retirement savings have gone into the latest big screen television, a big bass boat, and an annual seven-day cruise.

This all means to me that an entire generation is going to have a more difficult time retiring and taking care of themselves. Their children will be too busy working and spending to help care for them in what should be their golden years.

I realize that I practically stood alone among Democrats in Washington on many issues. Reporters who cover the Capitol and even in my native state where they've known me a long time refer to me as "maverick," like it's my first name. A word, which, by the way, Webster defines as "an unbranded range animal."

I love this great country. I've lived in it a long time. I've studied and taught its great history. And I know what has made it great and will keep it great. I know this deep in my soul. No amount of economic growth, global prosperity, and even international peace can overcome the darkness that results from the weakening of the American family. The family is where decency is born, where it is nurtured, and where it is sent out. If it doesn't happen there, it's probably not going to happen.

And Washington Doesn't Care. Oh, it says it does. But a wise man once said, "By their deeds ye shall know them." And there are no deeds coming out of Washington to help with the roots of this situation. A few bills introduced, a few speeches, a lot of posturing, but no results to change our direction.

Chapter 20

VOTING THE BIBLE

There's a great old hymn by that "sweet singer of Methodism," Charles Wesley, titled "Forth in Thy Name, O Lord." One of its stanzas begins, "The task Thy wisdom has assigned." That's one reason for this book. I consider it part of my assignment.

Part of the "task," I believe, is to point out how we have reached a critical juncture as a nation—that proverbial fork in the road. If we choose indecency in our courts, schools, entertainment, businesses, and in our nation's capital, we will do and go the way of the Roman and other civilizations that first rotted and then disappeared. If we replenish this deficit of decency with common sense, compassion, restraint, tough love, and truth, our example of liberty and freedom will become a beacon of hope throughout the world.

Our country is divided in ways few of us would ever have believed possible just a few years ago. We are divided over current issues, yet these issues are as old as the Bible itself. The admonition that "ye cannot serve God and mammon" hits us between the eyes and forces us to choose. I refer to (1) the public display of the Ten Commandments, (2) abortion on demand, (3) stem cell research, and (4) same sex marriage. All of these issues, to varying degrees, were part of the political discussions in the 2004 election and, without doubt, will be around when we vote our last time on this earth. Some have called these issues "voting the Bible"; others have referred to them as "voting righteously."

Briefly, I'd like to give you my thoughts on each one, not that my thoughts are any better or wiser than yours or anyone else. But I have hacked around in this jungle of life for a pretty good while, got lost more than a few times, and formed a few opinions.

First, displaying the Ten Commandments in a public place. I just don't get what is so complicated and controversial about this. We don't have a problem with "No Smoking" signs at the gas pumps. We don't have a problem with a "Sharp Curve" warning sign on a steep mountain road or a "School Crossing" sign and flashing lights near a school. In fact, we are thankful they are there to remind us. Can you imagine the chaos on our highways if there were no "Stop" signs? We have a history of appreciating things that are posted for our well-being and the protection of others. Often we complain when we are not warned. Why is this so different? To deny the posting of The Ten Commandments is to deny that we never need reminding on how to live a better life.

I'm not going to lay out a legal, academic, religious, or philosophical apologetic for why we need the Ten Commandments posted in public facilities. I don't have the ability to do so. I want to come at it from a more practical, man-on-the-street perspective.

Who can argue that following the Ten Commandments wouldn't make any one of us a better person? Who can argue that helping improve a person's character would not be good? We're not talking about some invasive public policy that requires one-hundred-page codebooks. Who could argue with don't steal, don't lie, and don't kill? What respectable and peace-loving faith could quarrel with such basic building blocks of character? Yes, following the Ten Commandments makes us better Christians, but following them also makes us better Americans, better neighbors, and better people. That is why the logic of taking down the Ten Commandments in public places escapes me. Would anyone argue that our character level is so great that following the Ten Commandments would have no effect on it? I don't think so.

There is an impressive carving on the beautiful marble walls of the U.S. Supreme Court in Washington, D.C. It is a dignified depiction of Moses handing down the Ten Commandments that God had proclaimed at Mt. Sinai. It is the perfect display for the highest court in our land, for it was the Ten Commandments that provided the foundation of not only our moral law but our judicial law as well. "Rules not only for action but for the government of the heart" was how President John Quincy Adams once described them.

How could those Supreme Court justices, who see and hopefully live by the commandments every day, rule that it is unconstitutional to display them in a public place? Isn't it right there in front of their noses? Larger than life, Moses is shown displaying them in one of the most public places in our nation's capital city. So why not in schoolrooms or city halls or courthouses across this Christian nation? It's crazy.

For years the Josephson Institute of Ethics has been tracking the rate of lying among American high school students. They do this every couple of years, and what they've found isn't pretty. In 1992, they surveyed twelve thousand high school students. Sixty-one percent admitted cheating on an exam at least once in the previous year. Guess what the numbers were ten years later? Would you believe 74 percent? That is astounding. These are the same kids who will be setting up shop in your towns and neighborhoods in a decade or so. These are the young men and women who will become our CPAs, our teachers, our doctors, and our lawyers. They are going to marry each other and raise families. So look out! I don't want a doctor operating on me who cheated to get through medical school, or to travel on a bridge built by an engineer who cheated on final exams.

While these numbers may be surprisingly high, I'll bet I'm not telling you anything you didn't already know. You may not have had the numbers behind the reality, but you know from your own experience that we now live in a land where people don't think twice about lying. It's been going on forever—since Adam's experience with Eve. But the data and our own experience shows it has now become a bigger and more pervasive problem than ever before. The deficit of decency in our country has helped produce a generation of children who assume lying to be a way of life without penalties.

My mother may not have provided a lot of the material things we take for granted today. I never tasted steak until I joined the Marine Corps. Our family never owned a car until I graduated from junior college. No indoor plumbing, no central heat, only a fireplace or wood heater. But I had a mother who used to tell us, "Tell the truth and bear the blame," and that if we cheated in school, "You'll only be cheating yourself."

For years, she sold magazine subscriptions and would accept only half the commission she was due. She sold her paintings dirt-cheap and her homegrown tomatoes for ten cents a basket. She would heap the baskets high with the biggest and best tomatoes she had to be sure she did not cheat someone. All of her dealings with people were that way, and I wish I could have lived my life half as well.

How will our children cope in a future where lying is the norm? And there is evidence that our willingness to lie is growing steadily. At the rate we're going, we'll be a nation of pure liars in a number of years. There is also evidence that lying crosses religious, cultural, geopolitical, and socioeconomic boundaries.

No one tells the George Washington cherry tree story any more. Many even think it silly.

In light of all this, would somebody then please explain to me why we can't hang "Thou shalt not bear false witness" on our walls and begin a conversation about honesty in our schools and class-rooms all across America?

The Ten Commandments should never have become a political issue. Can you imagine how silly it would seem if our Founding Fathers could hear us arguing about whether we have the constitu-tional right to hang the Ten Commandments on our public walls?

Who could ever have imagined that this would happen in the United States of America? Although I think it is important to select candidates who reflect your values, I also think it is less important to display the Ten Commandments than it is to obey the Ten Commandments. "Display and obey" is how I would sum it up. It's easy to support the Ten Commandments. It's a hard struggle to live the Ten Commandments. And if we don't live by them, our support won't matter anyway. It may even hurt.

Don't get me wrong. I want the Ten Commandments posted in our halls of justice and our schools. As a U.S. senator, I introduced legislation to do just that. But it won't amount to a hill of beans if you and I don't make it our priority to live them.

It took me a long time to take a stand against abortion, and this is something I will forever regret. For years after the *Roe v. Wade* decision in 1973, my position remained the same: "Leave it to the woman, her God, and her doctor." I did, however, favor a number of qualifications: no public funds should be used to pay for abortions; parents of minors who seek abortions should be notified; and no abortion should be performed after the first trimester. As governor I signed a bill outlawing the hideous and cruel procedure of partial birth abortion.

But then, about ten years ago, as my great-grandchildren began to arrive, I got around to the real question. I'll never forget when my grandson brought in a sonogram showing so very clearly his unborn daughter. I finally realized just how wrong I had been. What if those four precious great-grandchildren of ours had been aborted? I could not bear the thought. The more I read and pray, the more I regret that political position I so easily and thoughtlessly took for many years. And I am blessed that there is a forgiving God.

When I discuss the difficult issue with my friends, I tell them they must first decide this basic question: What is growing in the womb of a woman—a human being, a soul known to God, or is it a "fetus," just a blob of flesh? When you get right down to it, it seems to me that both science and religion describe it in the same way.

With modern science and sonograms, we now can see just how alive that little human being is. And, of course, the Bible has always been clear and direct.

In the 139th Psalm, David acknowledges to God, "You knit me together in my mother's womb....Your eyes beheld my unknown substance. In your book were written all the days that were formed for me, when none of them yet existed." And, of course, in Exodus 20:13, God says to Moses as he lists his Ten Commandments, "Thou shalt not kill."

Let's put this in perspective: We are fighting a war on terror to protect the innocent from wild-eyed, Islamic fundamentalists who seek to destroy our way of life. At the same time, the innocent unborn here in America aren't protected from today's culture of convenience and entitlement.

Mother Teresa once wrote, "The nation that will kill its child in the womb of its mother has lost its soul." That's heartbreaking. That's terrible. But this nation has also lost something that even the wise Mother Teresa never mentioned.

Think about these three major problems our country faces today: (1) Our Social Security system, which has served our elderly so well for more than six decades, will soon be bankrupt without significant changes. The single most important reason is that there are simply not enough young workers coming along, as they always did in the past, to support the current and future retirees. So the numbers don't add up. (2) We've got a shortage of workers in this country. That is why immigrants, even the illegal ones, have become necessary for our future workforce. There are simply not enough American workers. The numbers of supply and demand don't add up. (3) There's also a shortage of volunteers for our armed forces. Our ability to fight terrorists on two fronts, in two separate parts of the world, has been seriously diminished. Our troops are stretched thin in Iraq, Afghanistan, and on our own borders. Our National Guard has been deployed abroad, and if disaster or a major terrorist attack were to strike here at home, we could very well be overwhelmed and understaffed. As a result, there is concern, and some have even suggested that the draft could be reinstated.

How could this great land of plenty produce too few people? Here's why. Here's the brutal truth that no one dares to mention: we're too few in number because too many of our babies have been killed. More than 42 million babies since *Roe v. Wade*. If those murdered children had lived, today they would be defending our country, filling our jobs, and paying Social Security benefits. Sadly, 42 million were the baby boom that never blossomed.

Still, we do not raise our voices loud enough. Still, we watch as four thousand babies are killed every single day in America. One killed every twenty seconds. All these human beings with all their potential just flushed down the commode. It is unbelievable that a nation "under God" would do this. It's as unbelievable and as cruel as those innocents who were killed in the Holocaust. After those poor, innocent souls were gassed, starved, and burned, we built museums and monuments to honor them as we should. But today, our nation, which likes to think it has a heart, has torn millions of little bodies apart, cruelly butchered in the most horrible way imaginable. But no one talks of building a monument to this lost generation of Americans. And far too few even care enough to bring an end to this horror.

Could there be even a slight change in the national Democratic Party's opposition to abortion? Perhaps. It is not unlike the gun issue in 2000 when Democrats in states like West Virginia abandoned the Democratic Party. Generations of union members and other core party constituents voted for the Second Amendment and against their party. And the party, on this issue of abortion, is in an untenable position. There is simply no way to defend partial birth abortion. There is no way to defend using taxpayer's money to kill a baby. There is no way to explain, with any kind of logic, why a minor who can't buy beer or cigarettes can be taken to a clinic where her unborn baby is aborted without her parents ever being told that their grandchild has been killed.

If Democrats begin to support qualifications and limitations on abortion, it will be the beginning of something very important.

No one could be more interested in the potential of stem cell research than I. My mother died from Alzheimer's. I watched as the strongest, most determined human being I've ever known lived out her final years in a nursing home unable to recognize her family and friends. That alert, creative mind was gone. That sharp and quick tongue reduced to gibberish. And our son, Matt, who at five years of age was diagnosed a juvenile diabetic, has lived for forty-four years with a daily routine of insulin injections and tens of thousands of pin pricks for blood-sugar tests. Believe me, Shirley and I know of these cruel diseases, have long prayed for cures, and worked to raise money for more research.

So no one is more thankful that stem cell therapies promise to ease suffering and sickness for millions. The fact is they already are. The success of non-embryonic stem cells is overwhelming. There are many miraculous things being done today using stem cells simply taken from the patient's own body. Many sufferers of type 1 diabetes patients are now completely off insulin after receiving adult pancreatic cell transplants. Patients with heart disease and damaged hearts can be treated with their own stem cells. Some are even avoiding once needed heart transplants. CBS's *60 Minutes II* reported the story of a fifteen-year-old boy who was healed of sickle cell anemia from stem cells taken from umbilical cord blood. More than 20 million sufferers of multiple sclerosis have improved or avoided further decline after receiving an adult stem cell transplant.

These are therapies that are working and available now. All this, and not one unborn baby had to die. Not one embryo waiting to be born was harvested. To anyone who wants to read the Good Book honestly, the Bible is as clear on embryonic stem cell harvesting as it is on abortion. In vitro fertilization creates multiple embryos in a laboratory, and some are implanted in a woman's uterus. The others are frozen, used in experiments, or destroyed. This is the problem. Because everything God made is good and all of life is precious, the use of embryonic stem cells must be stopped. It is not a proper fate for a human being made in God's image.

Shirley and I are United Methodists. We believe in the social gospel so beautifully expressed by Jesus Himself: "Whatever you did for one of these least brothers of mine, you did for me." How can there be any question that Jesus meant the weakest, smallest, and most innocent of all humanity?

Which brings me to the fourth and most volatile issue dividing our nation today: For thousands of years in every continent on earth, marriage has been the bedrock of civilization. And in all those places and in all that time, marriage has always been defined as between man and woman. Whether Christian, Jewish, or Muslim—the definition is clear and universal.

Today, unelected activist judges, accountable to no one, reject that long history and are promoting a dangerous social experiment: same sex marriage. Over time, if not stopped, this practice will destroy the traditional family. It will affect our children in a terrible, harmful, and lasting way for generations to come.

The question is not whether our Constitution will be amended. That has already been decided. The question is who will amend it: activist judges or the voting public.

Now even the staunchest supporters of traditional marriage would be hard-pressed to claim that the institution of marriage today is perfect. In too many cases, it is not a paragon of virtue worthy of emulation. The easy, no-fault divorce laws enacted a few years ago have done irreparable harm. But marriage has always been a work in progress. I should know. Shirley and I have been working on ours every day for more than fifty years.

But I'm not just worried about the survival of marriage as an institution. I'm worried about the survival of our nation. A close examination of ancient Greece, Rome, Corinth, and Sodom and Gomorrah will show that homosexuality was an accepted practice in these cultures; but that same history also teaches us that there was always a cultural decline in the life of any nation that exchanged the sanctity of traditional marriage for the tyranny of unbridled sexual freedom. It doesn't take a historian to tell you that the death of morality in the life of a nation often leads to the death of a nation.

Ultimately, marriage ensures our future by protecting our children. Marriage encourages men and women who together create life to unite in a bond for the protection of children. It is the building block on which our society is based.

When the constitutional amendment defending marriage as a union between a man and a woman was being debated in Washington, fifty African American pastors from around the country tried to meet with the Congressional Black Caucus to discuss it. But the caucus slammed each door in their faces. One of those pastors was Dr. Creflo A. Dollar of the World Changers Ministries in College Park, Georgia. In a letter to the caucus, this great minister wrote eloquently on this subject.

> Our support for this amendment should not be viewed as homophobic, exclusionary, or discriminatory. The ministries represented here today extend the love of God to all people, including those who exemplify lifestyles that we don't agree with, and our doors are open to everyone.
>
> To attempt to categorize our collective stance in any other way is both irresponsible and inaccurate. This is not a Civil Rights issue, as many would have you believe, and attempts to frame it as such are an insult to the millions of Americans who have been the victims of actual discrimination in the past.

By protecting the institution of marriage, we protect the family, and to protect the family we must either work to pass constitutional amendments in every state or to our U.S. Constitution. We must organize our churches and civic clubs and hold our elected officials accountable. I believe anyone who holds elective office or hopes to has the obligation to state in unequivocal, unambiguous, plain-spoken words where they stand on this issue and how they will vote when the time comes.

Today, I'm sorry to say, too many of our politicians are hunkering down in the tall grass when it comes to this issue. They hope to go unnoticed because they don't want to take a firm position; they don't want to stand up and be counted. But that's what being a leader is all about—taking a position even if it is controversial.

Ask them to tell you plainly and forthrightly: Are you for it or against it? And if they start off their answer with gobbledygook or some fancy dance steps, stop them and ask them again. Keep asking until you get a straight answer, and then vote according to your conscience and sense of duty.

We have reached a point in our nation's history, and I suppose a point in each of our lives, when these issues matter more than ever.

Chapter 21

FREEDOM FROM SPEECH

One of our most cherished rights as citizens of this great nation is freedom of speech. The First Amendment to our Constitution guarantees us that freedom along with the right to worship as we please, freedom of the press, the right to peaceably assemble, and the right to petition the government for a redress of grievances. But nowhere in that document is there language relating to freedom *from* speech.

Perhaps there should be. I have always heard that "a man's freedom to swing his fist stops with my nose." Substitute "filth" for "fist" and "ears" for "nose" and you've got, "A man's freedom to spew filth stops with my ears." Or it should.

The great Supreme Court justice Oliver Wendell Holmes once said that "freedom of speech does not give the right to shout 'fire' in a crowded theater." Should it not then follow that free speech does not give one the right to shout the "F-word" over and over again in an adolescent's upstairs bedroom or proudly and profanely advocate murder and mayhem?

That is why I would argue that there is an inherent freedom *from* such speech. Doesn't it violate the law of disorderly conduct and decency? Doesn't it have the potential, just like "'fire' in a crowded theater," to stampede young people in the wrong direction and put them at risk? Today there are millions of young people who have become human septic tanks filled with violent and sexual messages denigrating God, country, and family.

Vile and violent words are piled, one on top of another, like an auctioneer's chant, numbing the senses as they find their way into those billions of synapses in a young person's brain that shape who they are, how they think, and what they will eventually do.

Nowadays, every vulgar outbreak, every crude remark, every sexually-explicit reference, and almost all other unacceptable conduct is overlooked by almost everyone as being simply an exercise of "free speech." Nowhere in the Bill of Rights is there a guarantee that protects us from this vast misuse of a precious freedom. Drafters of the Bill of Rights, and voters who ratified it, would turn over in their graves if they saw or heard the scum and filth that today some contend are guaranteed by the First Amendment to the Constitution.

I seriously doubt creators of the First Amendment intended "freedom of speech" to mean a naked dancer performing on a table in some topless joint, a disc jockey on some radio station in Florida openly discussing sex with a nine-year-old child, or the other vile acts of murder, mutilation, and mayhem blaring across our airwaves every day.

Yet that sordid behavior continues on with its unchecked constitutional seal of approval. Foul-mouthed talk-show hosts, rappers, and increasingly offensive television programming continues to destroy our sense of decency and decorum. Since when did the U.S. Constitution require parents to zealously examine television, radio, video, and CDs to protect their children from speech?

When Justin Timberlake pulled the tab on Janet Jackson during the Super Bowl, I became so incensed that I took the floor of the Senate and publicly denounced their behavior as proof of a "deficit of decency" that exists in America today.

What on earth were they thinking? The Super Bowl was supposed to be an American pastime—a time for parents and children to witness the best this country has to offer. But you can't just blame the stars for allowing such X-rated behavior to go on; they were merely responding to the lack of moral standards in the television and entertainment industry.

But can we truly blame the media and music moguls, many who are born to bottom feed? I don't think so. I think we all bear responsibility because we all bear witness to what happens when we turn our backs on, and fail to speak out against, such conduct. It is as if we have turned a collective blind eye to the trash talk and walk that is so pervasive in our culture today.

I thought I had heard and seen it all until I happened upon a hip-hop crapper by the name of Nelly. This so-called entertainer has a video called "The Drill," during which the star swipes a credit card through a young woman's back side. This disgusting act unleashes a tempest of men throwing money between women's legs and women simulating sex acts with other women. Should these acts and this video be protected by the Constitution? I think not. But I also think we haven't seen the last or the worst of it unless our political leaders, our churches, and our caring parents take a stronger stand and demand an end to such sordid and unacceptable behavior. Far too many churches are timid about this. Far too many parents want to be their children's best friend and not their guiding light. And it's not even on most politicians' radar screens. Washington Doesn't Care.

Years ago, movie critics panned Clark Gable's line, "Frankly, my dear, I don't give a damn," in the movie classic *Gone with the Wind*. They said it was too risqué even for the adults of that day. That was in 1939. The film's screenplay writers even suggested that Selznick change the script for censorship protection. They wanted Gable to say either, "Frankly, my dear, I just don't care," or "I wish I could care what you do or where you go, but frankly, my dear, I just don't care." Selznick obviously didn't give a damn. He allowed Gable to use the word that, in those days, was a certified "cuss word" as we mountaineers would say. I guess he never suspected that one little word would become the talk of the entire world.

Contrast that word with a recent song sung by teen idol Eminem titled "The Kids." Embodied within that one song, the rapper sings of cruelty to animals, drug use, explicit sex acts in a parking lot, murder, dismemberment, hiding a body for the "cops to find," the size of his penis, parental drug use, G-strings, and magic mushrooms grown in cow dung. Now imagine, for a moment, the millions of impressible adolescents trying to figure out who they are and where they are going in life as they listen to that toxic brew of trash.

Someone once said, and I'm sure we all agree, that if you want to change the world, you must begin with the children. It's just as certain that, if you want to guarantee the downfall of a nation, you must begin with its young people. It is decay from within that has destroyed many of the world's most prosperous nations. George Washington warned us of that in his farewell address when he cautioned that religion and morality are inseparable and that no true patriot would attempt to weaken the relationship between God and government.

I've always been a fan of country music. One of my favorite performers was the late, great Waylon Jennings. I liked him, not only because of his music, but also because he had the guts to stand up to the country music establishment in Nashville. Waylon refused to sing their Musak music and insisted that he write and sing his own. They rewarded him by shunning him and calling him an "outlaw." But Waylon fought back. In fact, he never stopped fighting back. In one of his later songs, Waylon sings: "Don't you think this outlaw bit has done got out of hand?"

Well, my answer to Waylon's question is pure and simple: Yes! I think this rap, hip-hop, gangsta music—or whatever you want to call it—has done got *way* out of hand. Rappers like Eminem, Tupac Shakur, and Ice Cube have become heroes to young Americans. The sad part is these so-called heroes live the lives they sing about while most Americans look on in silence. Hidden behind the catchy allit-erative lyrics of today's rap artists is an industry that feeds off a group of entertainers whose lives are even sorrier than their songs.

Tupac Shakur died at the hands of assassins in 1996, setting off a series of high-profile murders that has yet to end. Shakur became famous for his records exploring gang violence, drug dealing, police brutality, teenage pregnancy, single motherhood, and racism. He was by far the most popular rap artist of his time, so successful in fact that one of his rivals decided to have him killed following a Mike Tyson fight in Las Vegas. The supposed architect of his death was gunned down six months later in New York, the victim of bullets fired by a suspect who was also a rap singer. Shortly before Shakur was shot in Las Vegas, rapper Snoop Doggy Dog was charged, but not convicted, of murdering a rival gang member. Dog is still around today, singing his offensive rap music.

C-Murder, whose real name is Corey Miller, was indicted for killing a sixteen-year-old youngster with a shotgun blast to the chest. Eyewitnesses to the incident failed to testify because they feared Miller's violent retaliation. You see, at the time of the murder, Miller was free on a $100,000 bond on a previous charge of attempting to kill a nightclub owner. In June 2002, South Park Mexican Carlo Coy, was sentenced to forty-five years in prison for sexually assaulting a nine-year-old girl. But the most vicious crime occurred in May 2002 when rapper Big Lurch, Antron Singleton, was ordered to stand trial for killing and then eating—that's right, eating the flesh of a twenty-one-year old woman. There are count-less rap songs about "chopping" up people. These people belong in a penitentiary, not on a stage or over our airwaves with their words throbbing repeatedly in a young person's ears.

One of the industry's first successful rappers, Ice-T, gained fame with his 1992 release of a song titled "Cop Killer." Among other bits of advice he offered his listeners, Ice-T advocated murdering policemen. Since the release of "Cop Killer," he has become a movie star, performing in some fifty-nine films, and has made guest appearances on almost all of television's talk shows. Ironically, he now plays a police detective in the popular NBC television series, *Law and Order*.

By the way, don't confuse Ice-T with Ice Cube. The latter, in a song called "Black Korea," shouts, "respect the black fist or we'll burn your store down to a crisp." A few months after the release of "Black Korea," much of LA did in fact burn "to a crisp." Simple coincidence and convergence of other events such as the Rodney King beating, or a case of "shouting 'fire' in a crowded theater"?

The Ghetto Boys promote their work as "Gangsta Rap," and Time-Warner Communications markets this trash about a female being "ready" and "sweaty" and then urges murdering "that bitch like Freddy by chopping her up like spaghetti." Instead of suing McDonalds over a burn from a hot cup of coffee, Time-Warner should be prosecuted for accessory to murder anywhere a woman is murdered by someone who heard that song.

I could go on and on, but the point I want to make is simply this: Rap music is infiltrating the minds of today's young Americans by teaching lessons that violate every principle of moral conduct upon which this nation was founded. Supporters of these artists and their "legitimate" marketers, who make millions of dollars off of them, continue to maintain that the First Amendment protects their music. They also argue that rap music is an ethnic art form reflecting ghetto life; those who would criticize its content are dubbed "racists." Calling rap music an art form leaves me scratching my head in wonderment. How can anything that applauds violence, rape, murder, and sexism be an art form?

I have long been a student of ethnic music. I can recite the lyrics to many songs written and sung by mountain people during some of the hardest times any ethnic group has ever known. They recorded their misery with history, humor, tragedy, happiness, and religion. They chronicled the lives of great heroes, both real and fictional, like Davy Crockett and Uncle Pen. Loretta Lynn sings of the hard life of being a coal miner's daughter in the hills of Butcher

n Americans believe that rap music has a "destructive influ-
their communities. Only a handful—18 percent—of those
ved claimed it has a positive effect. Many admitted they
o's overall influence in the African American community
hat of the clergy, athletes, and teachers and is barely second
fluence of parents. And, sadly, far too many of them feel as
re unable to do anything about it.

they shouldn't have to go that road alone. No parent can
r their children's shoulders twenty-four hours every day to
lgment on what they see or hear. It's about time for the
st industry, cable networks, and record companies to bear
the responsibility by voluntarily adopting stringent codes of
hat protect the ears and eyes of young Americans. And if
n't muster sufficient backbone to adopt a code of ethics,
e should do it for them.

y should stop hiding like weak-kneed, scum-selling syco-
behind the First Amendment. Even the Federal
unications Commission, which took a longer nap than Rip
inkle, admits that obscene speech is not protected by the
ment and cannot be broadcast at any time. It's a shame that
those rare and precious few moments that FCC members are
y awake, they don't listen to Jerry Springer or Howard Stern
ar the filth that has to be bleeped out. I'll bet there's not a
teenager in America today who doesn't recognize bleeped
when they hear them. So why even bother bleeping them?

s a shame that our courts can't see our teens as they surf an
-full of Internet filth. Uncensored and graphic lyrics to rap
and videos can be easily accessed by any child in America with
imited computer skills. But statutes and prohibitions against
indecencies as defined by our courts do not apply to cable
rks and the Internet. But they should. And if they can't police
selves, someone should. Someone must! And if someone
't, our rapidly thinning moral fabric that once held this nation
er will disappear with disastrous consequences.

Holler in Kentucky; Dolly Parton gre
Mountains and wrote an epic about a
mother made for her daughter from r
over the years. She tells how the other k
but she was "proud as she could be."

Their songs tell stories of lost and r
and crossties that brought them home fi
of Old Joe Clark, Barbra Allen, and Sourv
mindful of their responsibilities to societ
effect their music had on those who hear
victimize, but to sensitize the young pe
their footsteps about the struggles they
still lives today in the hills and hamlet
endure forever as a symbol of the hard
reflect their struggle to rise above the pove

As a native Appalachian who knows on
to suffer ridicule and prejudice because of
when rappers hide behind claims of racism
this isn't about the color of one's skin. This
about moral decay. This is about making
Amendment. This is about what is good fo
most of all, this is about ridding our nat
growing day by day and will continue to pl
the guts to stop it.

The Reverend Jesse Jackson, the self-app
Black America, at one time seemed to agree
I'm going to clean up the reverend's quote to
words are as repulsive as the singers about
Here's what he said after my censorship: "Ar
who makes money calling our women bleeps
will have to face the wrath of our indignatior
ducked under the table.

Other African Americans agree. A poll
America's Political Action Committee last fall

Holler in Kentucky; Dolly Parton grew up in the Great Smokey Mountains and wrote an epic about a coat of many colors that a mother made for her daughter from remnants of cloth gathered over the years. She tells how the other kids at school made fun of it, but she was "proud as she could be."

Their songs tell stories of lost and regained loves; of steel rails and crossties that brought them home from jobs in faraway places; of Old Joe Clark, Barbra Allen, and Sourwood Mountain. They were mindful of their responsibilities to society and were sensitive to the effect their music had on those who heard it. They never sought to victimize, but to sensitize the young people who would follow in their footsteps about the struggles they had endured. This music still lives today in the hills and hamlets of Appalachia and will endure forever as a symbol of the hardships and sacrifices that reflect their struggle to rise above the poverty of their times.

As a native Appalachian who knows only too well what it means to suffer ridicule and prejudice because of one's culture, it pains me when rappers hide behind claims of racism. Let me make this clear: this isn't about the color of one's skin. This is about decency. This is about moral decay. This is about making a mockery of the First Amendment. This is about what is good for our young people. But most of all, this is about ridding our nation of a cancer that is growing day by day and will continue to plague us until we muster the guts to stop it.

The Reverend Jesse Jackson, the self-appointed spokesperson of Black America, at one time seemed to agree with me on this issue. I'm going to clean up the reverend's quote to the media because his words are as repulsive as the singers about whom he is speaking. Here's what he said after my censorship: "Anyone, black or white, who makes money calling our women bleeps and our people bleeps will have to face the wrath of our indignation." He said it and then ducked under the table.

Other African Americans agree. A poll conducted by Black America's Political Action Committee last fall shows that a majority of African Americans believe that rap music has a "destructive influence" in their communities. Only a handful—18 percent—of those interviewed claimed it has a positive effect. Many admitted they think rap's overall influence in the African American community exceeds that of the clergy, athletes, and teachers and is barely second to the influence of parents. And, sadly, far too many of them feel as if they are unable to do anything about it.

But they shouldn't have to go that road alone. No parent can look over their children's shoulders twenty-four hours every day to pass judgment on what they see or hear. It's about time for the broadcast industry, cable networks, and record companies to bear some of the responsibility by voluntarily adopting stringent codes of ethics that protect the ears and eyes of young Americans. And if they can't muster sufficient backbone to adopt a code of ethics, someone should do it for them.

They should stop hiding like weak-kneed, scum-selling sycophants behind the First Amendment. Even the Federal Communications Commission, which took a longer nap than Rip Van Winkle, admits that obscene speech is not protected by the amendment and cannot be broadcast at any time. It's a shame that during those rare and precious few moments that FCC members are actually awake, they don't listen to Jerry Springer or Howard Stern and hear the filth that has to be bleeped out. I'll bet there's not a single teenager in America today who doesn't recognize bleeped words when they hear them. So why even bother bleeping them?

It's a shame that our courts can't see our teens as they surf an ocean-full of Internet filth. Uncensored and graphic lyrics to rap songs and videos can be easily accessed by any child in America with even limited computer skills. But statutes and prohibitions against airing indecencies as defined by our courts do not apply to cable networks and the Internet. But they should. And if they can't police themselves, someone should. Someone must! And if someone doesn't, our rapidly thinning moral fabric that once held this nation together will disappear with disastrous consequences.

The United States Supreme Court has determined on several occasions that obscene speech is not entitled to First Amendment protection. In *FCC v Pacifica Foundation* back in 1978, the court held that the government, in this case the Federal Communications Commission, could constitutionally regulate indecent broadcasts. In that decision, the court upheld the commission's definition of indecency as being "language or material that, in context, depicts or describes in terms patently offensive as measured by contemporary community standards for the broadcast medium, sexual or excretory activities, or organs." But regrettably, it ends there.

Let me end with what the Focus on the Family folks found when they analyzed the *Nasty as They Wanna Be* album by the popular 2 Live Crew. It was found that the F-word was used 226 times on this single album. "B___h" was used 163 times. There were 87 descriptions of oral sex, and 117 times the male and female sex organs were graphically described. All on one album! An album that sold 1.7 million copies!

I think there should be a freedom *from* this kind of speech. I believe that the filth being pounded into the brains of our children from those harmless-looking CD players and the ever-present earphones that are growing out of our kids' ears is every bit as bad as shouting "fire" in a crowded theater. This type of free speech isn't free at all. It is costing us the very soul of this nation.

Chapter 22

INDECENT ROLE MODELS

For the last six decades of my more than seven-decade life, one of the most glorious days of the year was in early February when pitchers and catchers reported for spring training. I always felt that life was about to begin again.

Also, for most of that time, I kept *The Baseball Encyclopedia* within quick reach of wherever I worked or lived. For years, I kept a copy at my feet under my desk in the Georgia State Capitol. Often I would visit its dog-eared pages. For me it was therapy, similar to moseying around the stacks of a library or a really good bookstore.

You see, baseball is all about statistics. Batting averages, fielding averages, slugging averages, RBIs, ERAs, strikeouts, homeruns, wins, losses, saves, etc. You can argue about who was the greatest, which was the best team, etc., etc., but it still comes down to the "stats." And I used to drown myself in them.

Not anymore. I still love the game, still follow it closely, and will to my dying day. But seldom do I open up that magic book anymore. I took it out from under my feet and put it high on the top shelf with books that are seldom used. Those fascinating stats no longer fascinate. They have become meaningless. With steroids, the skills of the player are enhanced, and so are the numbers.

Look at them. In 1976, a homerun was hit every 65 plate appearances. In 2002, a homerun was hit every 35 plate appearances. Either the hitter or the ball or both were juiced. In more than 125 years of baseball, no one had ever come close to hitting 70 home runs in a season. But in 1998, Mark McGwire did with Sammy Sosa close behind. And in 2002, Barry Bonds, the BALCO Bomber, topped that with 73. Both are great athletes, no doubt about it. Bonds may well be the best baseball player who ever lived. But McGwire admitted to using androstenedione, better known as andros.

Bonds used a "supplement" called tetrahydrogestrinone or THG. It is called "The Clear," which is originally a hormone used to treat endometriosis in women. It takes only a few drops on the tongue. Another, "The Cream," which it is said Bonds used, is a mixture of testosterone and epitestosteune, a BALCO ointment rubbed on the body.

Now, some will claim these are "vitamins" or pseudo-steroids. Perhaps, but I'll tell you they were probably not the only substance being used. Human growth hormone (HGH) also can be injected, which builds up muscle tissue. Jason Giambi, it was reported, shot himself in the stomach with this concoction, which is used medically to make short kids taller.

So, with all these drops, injections, and creams, the stats no longer have the same meaning. Individual achievement, documented so carefully for decades, has been blurred forever. The users are stealing from those thousands who came before them and the vast majority of the players today who are steroid free.

Bud Selig, the timid commissioner who should have dealt with this years ago, and greedy owners have allowed—even encouraged—this to happen. They knew that baseball needed a "shot in the arm" (excuse the pun) after the baseball strike in 1994 outraged the fans and dropped major league attendance. They knew they could get these fans back with more homeruns going out of the ballparks.

Even more outrageous is the high-priced lawyer for the players' association, Gene Orza, who once said that steroids are no worse than

Two baseball players who did not need to use steroids, Hank Aaron and Mickey Mantle.

cigarettes. Selig, Orza, and Donald Fehr, director of the Major League Baseball Players Association, were not just the blind leading the blind. They were the backboneless leading the backboneless. They let the game and the players deteriorate into the indecent and scandalous situation it is in today. But with record crowds, making record money.

Fans, too, must bear some of the blame because they, like the owners, want to see those balls fly out of the park. And they buy the tickets to pay those enormous salaries.

The fact is that spectacular achievement has and can be accomplished without steroids. There is an old black and white photograph on my wall of a young Mickey Mantle grinning broadly and holding the baseball that he hit further than any baseball has ever been hit. It was hit off Washington Senators' pitcher Chuck Stobbs and landed 565 feet beyond home plate. Some argue that his blast out of Tiger Stadium in Detroit or the one off the façade of

Yankee Stadium were even longer. Mantle could also run from home to first faster than any other player, 3.1 seconds. The point is that Mantle used no steroids; he just had those Oklahoma zinc miner's genes.

Two of the most bulked up, juiced up behemoths to ever play the game, Ken Caminiti and Jose Conseco, both former league Most Valuable Players, said that between 50 to 85 percent of the players use steroids. Caminiti, by the way, died recently from a drug over-dose, which he said started with steroids. Jose Conseco recently published a book claiming to have witnessed several high-profile players using steroids, himself among them. Whatever it is, the game has been changed and these old stats in my much-used encyclo-pedia are out the window. By the way, steroids are not only used by hitters. Pitchers using them can speed up their fastball several miles per hour, and one's running speed can also be enhanced. Olympic sprinter Marion Jones won five medals in the Sydney 2000 Olympics and is also caught up in the scandal.

The new "rules" to curb steroid use are a farce. Furman Bishop, the highly respected Atlanta sports editor who has covered baseball for more than half a century, puts it best, "Major League Baseball has taken a swing at the steroid pitcher and fouled it off."

The very notion that a player has to be caught using four times before he gets a one-year suspension sounds like it should come off of one of Jon Stewart's *The Daily Show* headlines. A player should have one second chance and that is all. Two strikes and you're out should be the rule. In the Olympic organization, there is a two-year suspension for the first offense, not a weak ten days as in baseball. The rules don't even make it clear whether substances are actually banned. Glaringly absent are amphetamines and stimulants.

So that is why this lifelong fan was so pleased to see a president of the United States—one who knows the game—speak so candidly about the steroid problem and especially what it is doing to our youth who look up to these artificially bigger than life athletes as role models.

I was with President Bush on a trip to Philadelphia for the Army-Navy game the day after the scandal broke over Jason Giambi's grand jury testimony. Senator John McCain was along, and he couldn't quit talking about it. He was ballistic, and the next day on *Meet the Press* he threatened federal legislation unless Major League Baseball cleaned up its own mess. I'll never forget John's outrage: "I don't give a damn about Jason Giambi or Barry Bonds. I'm concerned about those high school kids who see these bulked up heroes and get to thinking that's the only way I'll ever be competitive. That's the only way I'll reach my dream."

Immediately, I knew he was right. And it hit home with me on a personal level, too. For I knew such a kid many years ago. Knew him well. Baseball was his entire life. He cared about nothing else. He ate, drank, slept, and talked it twenty-four hours a day. He could not get enough. He pestered everyone around him to hit him grounders, play pitch, or throw him batting practice. He would have given anything, and I mean anything, to have had more power in his bat, be physically stronger, or run the bases faster.

No one ever had a greater desire without the physical tools to go with it. He would be a grown man with kids of his own and a tour in the Marines before it would subside. That kid would have eaten dirt or human waste, stuck a needle in his leg, or gone to any length to have made himself stronger. He would not have hesitated to break the law. He would have traded thirty years of his life in a second to have even played Class D professional baseball.

So, McCain had got it. There are hundreds of thousands of kids today like I was long ago. In fact, *Newsweek* cited a 2003 analysis indicating that more than 300,000 students between the eighth and twelfth grades used steroids. Shockingly, one-third of them were females, and not all were jocks. They just wanted that impressive physical appearance they thought it would give them.

But when it comes to indecency, the juicers in baseball have to take a back seat to those horny hoopsters of the NBA whose moral compasses all point in the same direction and who have scattered fatherless babies from sea to shining sea.

Tattooed from head to toe like freaks in a side show, these thugs with their pierced body parts and immaculately kept cornrows thumb their noses at society, charge into the stands to beat up fans, rape women, smoke marijuana, raise dogs for fighting, and choke their coaches. Four out of ten players in the NBA have a criminal record. Often this behavior starts in college and gets worse as they make millions of dollars and quickly see that they can get away with anything. Put simply, they consider themselves above the law.

Or how about those National Football League role models, two out of ten with arrest records, bumping bellies and doing those "I'm the greatest" silly dances as if they had done something spectacular instead of a job they are paid well to do.

Two investigative reporters, Jeff Benedict and Don Yeager, in recent years have written at least three books that detail how out of control and lawless too many of today's professional athletes have become. Their titles include: *Pros and Cons: The Criminals Who Play in the NFL; Public Heroes/Private Felons;* and *Out of Bounds, Inside the NBA: Culture of Rage, Violence, and Crime.* These professional athletes are not held accountable because they are insulated by agents and high-priced lawyers. Winning games and making millions are more important than common decency. There's definitely a deficit here, and it's getting deeper. Someone has even put out an All-Slime team for the NBA.

Mike Tyson in professional boxing or the strutting, crude, profane thespians of unprofessional wrestling, I won't even go into. And, while not in the same category, I'm not going to forget Sammy Sosa and his corked bat. Just another way to cheat. Another way to gain an illegal advantage.

Just a "mistake," Sammy said. Mistake? Spread that on the grass and watch the grass grow green. Anyone who knows anything about the best hitters knows they have studied every centimeter of that piece of lumber before carrying it up to the plate. They guard and care for their bats like they do their family jewels.

I read where Bill Clinton told Sosa not to worry about it; the public would soon forget it. Just another example of feeling no shame for doing wrong. Maybe the public will forget, but history won't. How will time judge his great homerun chase with McGwire in 1998 or the fact that he is one of only nineteen men who have hit five hundred homeruns in a career? Perhaps more importantly is how his poor example may influence future generations.

Ironically, many of the players themselves would welcome additional testing. Curt Schilling and John Smoltz, two of the game's most dominating pitchers, have said that if the players were polled, a clear majority of them would support the program in place in the minor leagues. But the union's leaders, like defense lawyers defending criminals, vehemently oppose it. Smoltz, known for his outspokenness, has put it this way: "It's a matter of right or wrong, and steroids are wrong."

Put this man in as commissioner of baseball. In fact, put anyone in except who we have. Where is old Judge Kennesaw Mountain Landis when we need him? For those of you who don't know, Landis was the virtual dictator of the game after the 1919 Black Sox gambling scandal. He cleaned the game up, gave it an integrity it had lacked, and kept it that way until he died. Then, as in most professional sports, the inmates began to run the asylum. And think what the tickets cost! That's also indecent.

Chapter 23

WHO'S GONNA FILL THEIR SHOES?

Most serious country music fans and most serious country music singers consider George Jones to be the greatest of them all. (Except, of course, when it comes to Hank Williams—a legend for all times.) Known as "The Possum" and "No-Show" for missing a number of concert dates back in the 1980s, George has had a hit song each year in each of the last five decades.

Awhile back he had a hit song titled "Who's Gonna Fill Their Shoes?" It was a thing of beauty. The late Max D. Barnes and Troy Seals wrote it, and the chorus went like this:

> Who's gonna fill their shoes
> Who's gonna stand that tall
> Who's gonna play the Opry
> And the Wabash Cannonball
> Who's gonna give their heart and soul
> To get to me and you
> Lord I wonder, who's gonna fill their shoes.

George took their words and did his usual magic with that haunting baritone and aching heart, paying tribute to the great country singers of the past. But what really made the song so beautiful was that it took someone like the late, great Max Barnes to live it before it could ever be written. Max was born in 1936 in a place called Hardscratch, Iowa. You can't make something like that up. Max left school at the age of sixteen to pursue a career in music.

He married the lead singer of his band and did whatever he needed to in order to support his family and feed his dream. At various times, Max was a truck driver, lathe operator, carpenter, deckhand, bartender, carnival worker, car salesman, and foreman of a lamp factory. Obviously, Max did what ever it took. And then finally he became a well-known and successful country songwriter. He recorded a few himself, but they never really took off.

But, you see, it takes someone who's got their own blisters and calluses from working at it so long to wonder out loud so poignantly about the future. It takes someone who did whatever it took to get the job done to recognize that those kinds of folks are getting harder and harder to come by these days. "Who's Gonna Fill Their Shoes?" is a great country song for sure. It's not, however, just a country song. It's about *a* country. It's about our country. It's about America.

The America we know today was built on the backs of brave, strong, and decent men and women who, like Max, did what it took. The sociologists call them the Builder Generation. I'm always interested in how sociologists love to lump people into groups in an effort to explain who and why we are. Then, after the lumping they do the labeling—Baby Boomers, Busters, Generation Xers, Net Generation. I can't keep up with them all. Sometimes it seems like we're being observed and classified like mice in a laboratory.

But the sociologists got it right when they named those of us born roughly between 1910 and 1945 the "Builder Generation." The Builder Generation fought communism, rebuilt the economy and a banking system after the depression, dealt with Hitler, Hirohito, and Mussolini.

The Builder Generation formed the civic backbone of communities that we now take for granted. They helped build hospitals, organized 4-H chapters, and made donations to build churches and expand their outreach. They rationed gas, bread, sugar, and cheese. Many of the women left their aprons at home and went to the assembly line to free a man to fight. My mother was one of those. "I'm going to be working, building B-29's," she told her two young children. America and the world called on them for more than their fair share. And when the call came, they stood up and said, collectively, "You can count on me. Where am I needed?"

These were the builders. Four in particular come to mind, men who were my closest friends and played important roles in my life. In fact I can't imagine my life without them.

There was Arnold Keys, who came back from the battlefields of Europe, took off his uniform, and started the first little league baseball team in our community. I was his second baseman and later his teammate, but I learned much more than baseball from this witty and wise philosopher of life.

Guy Puett landed on Omaha Beach in the first wave on D-Day, June 6, 1944, fighting his way through France and marching proudly under the Arch de Triumph when Paris was liberated. Then he came back to the mountains of North Georgia, took off his uniform, and became an educator in a place and at a time when education was not that highly prized. He also became one of my closest friends and taught me more about politics than James Carville, Paul Begala, and Dick Morris combined.

Ray Taylor left Hiawassee and traveled to the other side of the world in the India-Burma theater with the Army Air Force. He then came back home, took off his uniform, and shaped our country in so many positive ways. He was a Michelangelo with a bulldozer, who leveled hills, filled gullies, and built parks, roads, and bridges. Later he was a progressive county commissioner and the friend who paid my qualifying fee to run for the state senate.

Dr. Charles Van Gorder flew in a motorless, wooden glider on the night before D-Day behind enemy lines, risking all to set up medical stations. Tom Brokaw devotes one of the first chapters of *The Greatest Generation* to this good doctor and his partner Dr. John Rodda, who were captured by the Germans and spent time in a German prison camp. Then he came back home, took off his uniform, and built a little clinic in the North Carolina village of Andrews, where he delivered our first son.

You don't forget Builders and friends like these. They're all dead now, gone to what I know was a just reward, but they will always live in my heart, for my home area would be much less without them.

These Builders, and thousands like them all over this nation, went through a lot, some of it exciting and some of it dull and unfashionable by today's standards. But their experiences and their productivity shaped an entire generation. Builders were adults before television was invented. Their childhood and teen years were spent listening to family members tell stories on the front porch or by the fireplace. Most Builders are natural storytellers, and they entertained each other. They gathered around the family radio for entertainment and listened to ball games, music, and Fred Allen, Fibber McGee and Molly, and Jack Benny. Builders knew how to sit still and listen and use their imagination.

Builders lived through the Depression and are warily suspicious of buying anything on credit, especially things that aren't a necessity. The check cashing loan shark businesses of today wouldn't have a chance with this bunch. Builders knew the importance of not just their own savings, but of America's savings.

It took civic pride, trust, and even faith in one another to put money back in the bank after the crash of 1929. The industrial revolution that led to today's manufacturing-supported economy was possible because the Builders worked their shifts without complaint and with honor. As a generation, the Builders were loyal to their families, supported their leaders, and gave without asking for more in return. Their word was as good as money in the bank.

Could I be guilty of romanticizing the past? Perhaps. But you don't have to be a Builder to look around and recognize that civic pride is dying, a sense of duty is plainly undernourished, and common decency is rapidly disappearing. George and Max might've put it best when they asked, "Who's Gonna Fill Their Shoes?"

Who will be our builders of tomorrow? Who will answer the call and do the dutiful and decent thing? Having to ask questions like these worry me. That's why I'm worried about America. Because, you see, to use another line from an old Max Burns song, "This Ain't My First Rodeo."

The Builders understood and were ready to do their duty so that freedom could be enjoyed. Instinctively, they knew freedom wasn't free, that it had a price. Sometimes a steep one. The Builders were hung up on responsibility so those that followed could have it better. They felt they owed that to their children and grandchildren. There wasn't time for silly protests. They had no time for marching, burning bras, and waving placards. There were babies to feed and cars to build. Yes, they knew that freedom, liberty, and autonomy weren't cheap or a given. A crazed mustached Nazi across the pond was bent on annihilating the possibility of that kind of freedom. Threats to freedom weren't an abstraction for them. They were real. They heard Edward R. Murrow talk about it on the radio every night in that serious hushed tone of his.

But, at least it seems to me, each generation has taken a larger and larger step away from the legacy of the Builders. And what do we have to show for it? Record household debt. A divorce rate that hovers above 50 percent on a regular basis. Kids killing kids in our streets, filling their bodies with dope and their heads with filth.

Somehow we must restore what the Builders knew and lived by: that the kind of freedom upon which our Republic stands is joined at the hip with an equal sense of responsibility. Freedom without responsibility is a gas pedal with no brake.

So who is gonna fill their shoes? Surely Moses asked questions such as this. Despite his advice and example, Moses couldn't make the Hebrews stay with God. Even though God had delivered them and promised them a new land flowing with milk and honey, they got bored. They got tired. They were divided. They started to grumble. They needed some entertainment. They wanted to party. They began to forget who it was that had claimed them. The Bible tells us that they pooled their gold in protest and made for themselves an idol in the shape of a calf, I guess to be used at some Halftime Show. How pitiful. Yes, Moses must have had his doubts. He knew he wouldn't make it to see the promised land, but he trusted in God that the people could get there without him. Coming down from the mountain after having received the law, he must have wondered what a mess things had become.

But, remember, as Paul Harvey likes to say, "the rest of the story." You see, there was Joshua. Where Moses left off, Joshua picked up. Joshua, standing on what God had accomplished through Moses, heard the call of duty, accepted it, and led the Hebrews to defeat Jericho and enter the promised land.

Today's Joshuas may well be those marvelous and brave men and women in uniform who heard a call of duty and answered it.

Chapter 24

VICTIMS-R-US

"The devil made me do it." With those simple words, Geraldine Jones (a.k.a. Flip Wilson) once made nearly every American household laugh. The Flip Wilson show was one in a line of entertaining, hour-long variety shows that America enjoyed in the 1950s–1970s.

I wish we had more of them today. Parents and grandparents these days have to keep fingers on the remote even during primetime family hour programming. Who knows when a mammary gland will jump out or foul language "slip" through the censors? And how many of us can stomach the silly plotlines of today's sitcoms? Most are as ignorant as they are foul. Families back then could actually watch something on television and not have to be their own FCC. Doris Day, Tony Orlando, Mac Davis, Glen Campbell, Carol Burnett, Sonny and Cher, these were the family entertainers of yesteryear. Each of them was great, but none made a footprint quite like Flip Wilson.

"The devil made me do it" became a part of our shared lexicon, universally understood as a hilarious and outrageous attempt to blame someone else for our own lapses in judgment. The fact that Flip was probably the first primetime comedian to make his way into our living rooms dressed as the wife of a prominent minister helped, too. Geraldine made us laugh because no matter how much of the good preacher's money she spent on her latest dress, it was the devil that had made her do it.

When Flip Wilson gave us those words, it was ludicrous to think that someone could distance themselves from their actions. There was humor in the notion that someone could, using their own free will to do a thing and then dismiss themselves from it. It just wouldn't be funny today, and, for me, there's nothing funny about that.

Geraldine has been rendered obsolete because the blame game is deeply woven into our national fabric. She's no longer funny because we have made a habit of refusing to take responsibility for our actions. We have in some odd and perverse manner become a culture that creates rather than recognizes victims. Let me try to explain. There are folks in our culture who genuinely need and deserve help. Once upon a time, America was a place that, if you needed a helping hand, the good folks of our communities and towns were not only willing but received pleasure from helping. If you were in a ditch and couldn't get out, there were plenty who would happily grunt, push, pull, whatever it took to get you out. But today America is turning into the kind of place where, if someone digs a ditch and hangs a nail doing so, he becomes a victim and somehow feels the right and obligation to sue the shovel maker and maybe even the maker of the dirt. (But, of course, that can't be done because the Lord isn't recognized by today's courts.)

We've gone from a place that is willing to help true victims to a place where too many folks are looking for ways to become victims with the promise of huge cash settlements.

In the Bible there's a story of a young man who followed every rule in the book. He asked Jesus what else he must do to gain eternal life. Jesus simply answered, "Go and sell whatever you have and give it to the poor." Matthew writes that "When the young man heard this, he went away grieving, for he had many possessions." The young man in this gospel story had the opportunity and the means to go after what he longed for. But he chose otherwise. He chose to go back home and find shelter under his circumstances. By today's standards, he should have sued Jesus for placing such a difficult choice in front of him.

Geraldine is no longer funny because America has become a place where, when something of our own making turns out bad, we find someone to blame; and then we sue them. It's a shame to even have to think such a thing, let alone write about it. But what else are we to say or think about the lengths some folks will go today to achieve victim status and a fat check in the mail.

Take for example the man who sued Taco Bell for serving him a beef burrito when he had ordered a bean burrito. The man claimed to be a devout Hindu and said it had caused him "emotional distress and medical and travel expenses" since he had to travel to India to bathe in the Ganges River and be purified. The man had really not eaten the beef burrito, only bit into it, and when Taco Bell had offered a quick bean substitute, he refused.

States are always being sued. The state of Michigan was sued for one million dollars by a man who caught a cold in the drafty rotunda of the state capitol. Perhaps he should try our nation's Capitol—no shortage of hot air there!

In Illinois a prison inmate was denied the right to practice religion in the nude and sued the state.

Another man, a convicted rapist, sued the hospital where he had raped a patient in her bed. He maintained the hospital should have provided better protection for patients and asked $2 million for pain and suffering.

A strip club in Orlando, Florida was sued by a quadriplegic because it did not provide wheelchair access to the lap dancing area.

A man who was circumcised as an infant as requested by his parents actually claimed in a court of law that he, and all other males after the age of eighteen who dislike having been circumcised, should have the right to sue.

Kellogg Company and Black & Decker were sued when a couple in New Jersey claimed their house burned down when a Pop-Tart got caught in the toaster. At least that's what they "thought" had happened, because they had left the house as it was being heated.

Coaches, especially, cannot escape. There have been hundreds of suits against them. A softball coach was sued in Pennsylvania by one of his players for $700,000 because, the player maintained, his bad coaching kept him from receiving a college scholarship. In Chicago, when a star player was kicked off the high school basketball team for his second DUI, he sued the school for reinstatement and for $100,000.

There are hundreds, indeed thousands of examples just as absurd, just as wacky that take up court time and waste our taxpayer's dollars. The get rich quickly, victim mentality is a cancer woven throughout the fabric of our society and has been knit one stitch at a time.

Take, for example, the institution of welfare, which has created generations of folks who somehow think they are entitled to a certain amount of protection and support regardless of the amount of work, or lack thereof, they perform. A welfare state mentality encourages a person, I believe, to go from "I think I'll choose X" to "I think I'll sue some company because X didn't turn out too good." Welfare was conceived as a way to help out those who truly need it, and doing so makes life better for all of us. But the unfortunate and unintended consequence is an America where some are willing to hunt for the perfect "workmen's comp" moment. The Ralph Nader crowd has been another factor, I think. OSHA as a phenomenon has sustained and grown the idea that corporations should be responsible for the lack of judgment, laziness, or carelessness of its customers, or pay the price. The general decline in the old-fashioned value of an honest day's work for an honest day's pay has created an acceptance of the "find a shortcut to wealth" syndrome. Why work if one can put the squeeze on some big company that's loaded with money?

Regardless of who is to blame or how we got here, it is critical that we examine how this mentality will impact our ability to remain the home of liberty and freedom. We are forced to consider how self-determination and the ability to work, spend, and worship as we choose may change or diminish. How the Statue of Liberty's eternal flame could flicker or be extinguished altogether by the blast of a terrorist bomb. Terrorism, international unrest, once-close international allies now sullen, full of pride and prunes, refusing to do their fair share in making the world a better place for freedom and democracy could bring about an old world order of tyranny and evil.

This is big stuff. It takes big and courageous hearts to tackle such things. But how in God's name are we going to prevail if we can't muster enough courage to admit that when we eat too much fast food junk we get fat, or if we smoke too many cigarettes we may get lung cancer? When will we find the spine to admit that so many of these things are no one's fault but our own?

Tort reform advocates are only addressing part of the problem by seeking to curtail easy money made by those who clog our courts and help burn taxpayer dollars. Frivolous lawsuits are only the tip of the iceberg if you ask me. For those who seek a free ride by playing the blame game, keep it up if you must, because the bridge you are building won't quite get us to the other side. Because we don't have a future if my future is the only one I care about.

I wish Flip Wilson was funny again.

Chapter 25

TAKING CHRIST OUT OF CHRISTMAS

After the 2004 election and during the Christmas season I came across a new word: "Christianphobia." I turned to my trusty Webster's Dictionary, the one that claimed to have "more than 1,000 new words and meanings," for a complete and unabridged explanation. But I couldn't find the word anywhere.

While I was in Mr. Webster's learned pages, I did check "phobia" and found what I had expected—"persistent illogical fear." Oh, I said to myself. Now I get it. "Christianphobia" is an illogical fear of Christ whose advocates won't go away. The word made sense because it described those who want Jesus Christ removed from our schools, public buildings, and daily lives. It dawned on me that the Christian phobes had a lot to fear, especially during the Christmas season.

After all, more than 90 percent of this vast country was gearing up to celebrate the birthday of Christ. And if Christmas weren't enough to send the secularist and ACLU crowd into a complete tailspin, Easter would be just around the corner. The birth of Christ was one thing, but a full-fledged holiday to celebrate His resurrection and assurance of everlasting life, that would surely send this bunch into hysterics and lawsuit-happy overdrive. One thing was for certain; if you had a persistent or illogical fear of Christ, America was not the place to spend your Christmas holiday.

It was Christmas 1940, as an eight-year-old boy, that I first came to understand the meaning of taking Christ out of Christmas. Since my father had died when I was seventeen days old, it was left up to my mother to raise my sister and me. She built us a house with rocks she helped gather from a nearby creek and once divided our living room with chicken wire and placed a brooder in the corner to raise chickens until they were frying size and could be sold. But no matter how difficult things might've been, when Christmas Day arrived we huddled together around the fireplace she had created with those rocks—in shapes and patterns that only an artist could design—and thanked God for giving us His only Son.

I remember that Christmas of 1940 distinctly because it was one of the few times in my mother's life when she roared like a lion. It all started when someone in the valley had decided to update their Christmas decorations with a sign that read "Merry X-mas." To her, that simple sign was a serious slight to the Son of God who had died on the cross for our sins. Christmas, after all, was supposed to be a celebration of His birth. When she saw that sign, she said to us, "Merry X-mas? That's taking Christ out of Christmas. That's profane!"

As I sit down to write these words, sixty-five Christmases have passed, and three additional generations of Millers have come into this world and sat by that same fireplace on Christmas Day. As I write, Christmas is once again approaching, and the old blue mountains are frozen white by a morning freeze. It doesn't take much for me to imagine the smell of country ham, sausage, homemade applesauce, and biscuits coming from these rock walls or the glorious sounds of Christmas carols booming up from Brasstown Valley. Soon, our children, grandchildren, and great-grandchildren will arrive with their families and sometimes extended families and friends, and it will turn into standing room only. But it wasn't always

Dwight R. Lee, an economist who once taught at the University of Georgia, has put it much better than I can.

> There is no avoiding the fact that liberty will perish if the exercise of liberty is not tempered by an ethic of individual responsibility. The affirmation of this fact is the ethical responsibility of those of us who cherish liberty and understand the fragile foundation upon which it stands.

Look across America. Does it need more rules or more liberty? Does it need more laws or more responsibility? We're facing challenges today our Founding Fathers never dreamed of. But because of their great wisdom, the U.S. Constitution is more than ready to take on the challenges. As America keeps reshaping herself for this new millennium, her basic foundations must not waver. As we strive to keep America proud, strong, and free, we need to be asking the basic question of liberty. When standing at a crossroads where it becomes unclear how to respond to a new idea, proposal, or law, we must ask this simple but critical question: is it liberty or is it license? Does this build upon a sense of freedom and restraint that we know as liberty? Does it provide opportunity and require responsibility? Or does it depend upon a selfish sense of me, autonomy without consequence?

Peter Marshall was an immigrant who landed on Ellis Island in 1927. God called that great man to minister where he was, and that he did. He was a pastor in Atlanta, Georgia, where he became famous for a Depression-era sermon called "Singing in the Rain," of all things. Marshall went on to become the great chaplain of the United States Senate. From there his prayers to God touched the world, for they inspired the leaders of his nation to strive for something greater than themselves.

Peter Marshall's prayers, like truth, have an eternal quality. Although he died suddenly in 1949, this prayer of his still calls us to a place of deeper faith and love of the liberty for which God made us.

> Lord Jesus, thou who art the way, the truth, and the life; hear us as we pray for the truth that shall make all free. Teach us that liberty is not only to be loved but also to be lived. Liberty is too precious a thing to be buried in books. It costs too much to be hoarded. Help us see that our liberty is not the right to do as we please, but the opportunity to please to do what is right. (Peter Marshall, before the U.S. Senate)

THE SUNSET

*I have a long life to look back upon
and an eternity to look forward to.*

— John Jay

Although retired, I'm far from finished promoting this country, its values, and its faith. I will continue in the way that I began: remembering where I came from, who I am, and being ready to answer the call of God to do what is right and just and good for America. After all, the hope of a better future is why young people dream dreams and old men plant trees.

Chapter 27

GUS, WOODROW, AND "DARK THIRTY"

I read somewhere recently about a nine-year-old Border Collie in England that has a vocabulary of two hundred words and can learn new words after hearing them only once. Border Collies are smart. My grandsons have two, and they are a special breed, no doubt about it, but high maintenance. If they were human beings, we'd call them workaholics.

Which brings me to my two furry friends, Gus and Woodrow, Yellow Labrador Retrievers who are pretty smart themselves, but about 190 words short of their Border Collie cousins. They are up in a flash when they hear "walk," "treat," or "let's go." They're also not bad with "sit," "stay," and "down." But that's about it. Some of my friends say I trained and taught them like recruits at boot camp, but those who say it don't really know anything about boot camp.

My dogs are eight years old, and if they live four more years and I live four more years, then I figure we'll hit age seventy-seven together, seven years being a dog year. I hope we can do that. What a birthday it would be.

They're named after two of the most compelling characters in recent fiction, Gus McCrae and Woodrow Call, the two colorful, old Texas Rangers in Larry McMurtry's Pulitzer Prize winning novel *Lonesome Dove*. It's a book that I've kept in close reach for several years. I turn to it frequently to read favorite familiar passages, like toward the end when Gus escapes the Indians but loses a leg and is dying in Miles City, only a few miles from their final destination. Captain Call comes as soon as possible and can't resist scolding his old friend: "You always was careless. Pea said you rode right over the hill and into them. I've warned you about that very thing a thousand times." Gus gives this great reply: "Yes, but I like being free on this earth. I'll cross the hills when I please."

The doctor believes Gus could live if his other leg were amputated, but Gus will not allow it and holds a pistol on his old friend when it is suggested, explaining why he needs at least one leg. "I might want to kick a pig, if it aggravates me." He elaborates, "You don't get the point, Woodrow. I've walked this earth in my pride all these years. If that's lost, let the rest be lost with it. There are certain things my vanity won't abide."

Woodrow answers bitterly, "That's all it is, too. Your goddam vanity."

My dogs are exactly like their namesakes. Woodrow likes to go out by himself, a loner. Gus described it in the book: "Woodrow likes to be out where he can sniff the wind. It makes him feel smart." One of their sidekicks, Pea, put it simply: "The Captain likes to go off."

Gus, on the other hand, is always under my feet. He sleeps on the floor by the side of my bed as close to me as he can get and will lay snuggled beside me on the floor for as long as I will stay there. He wants lots of attention, as Captain Augustus McCrae did—that vanity, I guess. He is full of little games he wants to play. A spirit who wants to be free on this earth.

A few years ago, a friend, knowing how I love these dogs, gave me this statement. It's anonymous.

God summoned a beast from the fields and He said:

Behold man created in my image.
You shall protect him in the wilderness,
Shepherd his flocks, watch over his children, and
      accompany him wherever he may go, even into
      harm's way.
You shall be his companion, his ally, his slave.
I will endow you with these traits uncommon to other
      beasts:
faithfulness, devotion, and understanding, surpassing
      those of man himself.
Lest it impair your courage, you shall never foresee your
      death.
Lest it impair your loyalty, you shall be blind to the faults
      of man.
Lest it impair your understanding, you are denied the
      power of words; your eyes shall convey the truth
      of your heart.
Lest man's attachment to you grow too great, the span of
      your life shall be brief.
Walk by his side, sleep in his doorway, forage for him,
      ward off his enemies, carry his burdens, share his
      afflictions, love him, and comfort him.
And in return for this, man will fulfill your needs and
      wants, which shall be only sustenance, shelter,
      and affection.
So be silent and be a friend to man.
Guide him through the perils along the way to the land
      that I have promised him.
This shall be your destiny and your immortality.

So spoke the Lord.

I've never known exactly where the hot-temper genes in my DNA came from. I just knew they were there. From the time I was a kid through the sports period in my young life, to an adult and then an old man, it has been one of my worst features. Next to impossible to control. It would come quickly like a summer storm, and after the thunder and lightning, it would go just as quickly.

James Carville, the CNN political analyst and Democrat partisan who helped me be elected governor in 1990 (and I would not have won without him), once said of me, "Even when Zell has Alzheimer's he will remember every single person who slighted him."

There's some truth to that, I admit. The day after I signed on as a co-sponsor to the first Bush tax cut, James demanded I refund the $1,000 contribution he had made to my 2000 campaign for the U.S. Senate. The check was in the next mail. And a new little wrinkle went into the folds of my brain to remain there forevermore.

But the hot temper I felt when it first happened has long subsided. In fact, in my daily prayers, along with my thanks for all the blessings my Lord has given me in such abundance over the years and the pleas to watch over my loved ones, I never fail to pray for my temper to be blunted and the profane words used automatically and in conversation for more than half a century to be cleansed. I'm not there yet in either of these, but the Lord is not through with me yet and I'm trying. I'm trying hard.

But, as I've said, I don't know where it came from. What I've heard and seen of my daddy's folks was that they were unusually gentle, low-keyed people who never raised their voices. My mother's people, the Bryans, were much more fiery and demonstrative. But not my mama. She was strong, very opinionated, but not loud at all.

I guess that is why I remember so clearly, although sixty-five years have now passed, seeing my mother bristling and red-faced with anger rush off our back porch to confront a man walking down the dirt road beside our house. She marched up to him, blocking his path so that he had to stop and, as the saying goes, *got in his face.*

It had to do with a part-time job he had given her, one that was needed and had come at a good time for our struggling family. I didn't hear all the words, and the conversation was definitely one-sided, but I did hear her last words as she turned abruptly and marched proud and erect, back to our house, without a job.

I remember the words clearly to this day, not just because of the vehemence in which they were spoken, but because of the glorious colorfulness of their expression. Before she stomped off, a single mother of two with no job, she spit out this line: "I will not be a cat's paw for your rotten politics."

Over the past four years serving in the U.S. Senate, I've often thought of those words so plainly expressed by my mother long ago. There is no doubt that many in the Democratic Party wish I had stayed in the North Georgia mountains, in the house that my mother built, with Gus and Woodrow, and lived out the rest of my days in quiet anonymity. I can't help but think of the great Irish bard Dylan Thomas and his immortal advice: "Do not go gentle into that good night, old age should burn and rave at close of day; Rage, rage against the dying of the light." I certainly couldn't be accused of "going gently." But it also wasn't my intention of taking on the national Democratic Party's leadership.

When Georgia governor Roy Barnes, a strong Democrat whom I always believed had great national potential, strongly urged me to accept his appointment to fill the seat of the late, great Senator Paul Coverdell, I had no idea the result would be a long and rancorous divorce with the party for which I had worked so long and so hard. And if my actions offended him, I am deeply sorry.

To the national Democratic leadership who warmly welcomed me and contributed to my campaign, I regret it turned out as it did. I certainly did not anticipate or plan it that way. But I also would never apologize for telling the truth or voting for what I thought was good for my state and nation. I could never become a "cat's paw" for the rotten, ultra-liberal-special-interest brand of politics I was asked to support. I want Washington to care, for the good of the people of this great nation.

The chairman of the Georgia Democratic Party has been quoted as saying, "Something went bad wrong." It did. It has. I've tried to explain it now in two books, and many still don't seem to get it. This is not the same Democratic Party I worked for all those years. It is no longer the party of Harry Truman and John F. Kennedy. And it's not the party of Zell Miller.

Shirley, my companion, comptroller, critic, and crutch for the past fifty years continues to fill that job description. Even more a mountain person than I, we stay busy working, reading, and traveling together. The mother lion of our rather large pack, she is the one we all go to with all our problems great and small. She dispenses advice, help, discipline, and unqualified love—sometimes the "tough" kind—to all of us around the clock, seven days a week. The

Celebrating fifty-one years of marriage and still counting.

Lord surely blessed us when He sent her our way. They say men often look for wives like their mother. I'm sure I did and I was doubly blessed when I found one.

So now, as the pages turn on the final chapters of my life, I remember how it was in that first chapter of my life, growing up in that remote valley, in the house my mother built for us.

On early summer nights—at "dark thirty," as we called it before the TVA dammed up the Hiawassee River and brought electricity to our valley—after the moon had come up over Double Knobs and the lightning bugs were blinking, while the frogs croaked down at the creek and the katydids sang, and every once in a while a whippoorwill's lonesome cry could be heard, I remember, after my mother had finally quit working and was getting us quiet and ready for bed, we'd play a game.

The game would start when the headlights of a rare car would penetrate the darkness, maybe once every half-hour, on the narrow strip of cracked asphalt across the deep ditch in front of our house. We'd stare as the headlights would disappear and then reappear as the car made its way around the steep curves and finally across Brasstown Mountain. We'd count and we'd see how long it took from the time it went by the house until its taillights disappeared through the distant gap and it was no longer a part of that one and only world I knew.

It was often at this time that my mother would laugh and say, "You know what's so great about this place? You can get anywhere in the world from here."

This old world has turned many times since I first traveled that narrow road through the gap and out of Brasstown Valley. It has been a long road with many twists and turns, ups and downs, bumps and wrecks. A road that finally carried me twice to the highest office of the ninth largest state in the nation, to the United States Senate, to all the continents and famous cities of the world, to the Oval Office, and onto Air Force One, to Madison Square Garden where I twice spoke to millions of people through a medium unknown and unimagined when I was a child watching those cars and playing that game.

And so I close my career, knowing that once again my mother has been proven right. One could get anywhere in the world and back again from that little mountain valley. And I've always wanted that to be true for every child in America.

APPENDIX

RNC KEYNOTE ADDRESS
FIRST DRAFT (AUGUST 9, 2004)

Since I last stood in this spot, a whole new generation of the Miller family has been born: four great-grandchildren. Along with all the other members of our close-knit family, they are my and Shirley's most precious possessions. And I know that's how you feel about your family also.

Like you, I think of the future of my children and their children. I think of the promises and the perils they will face.

Like you, I believe that the next four years will determine what kind of world they will live in, what kind of future they will have with its hard challenges, our fanatical enemies, and often timid allies.

Together, we ask which leader is it today that will give America the best chance to preserve our freedom, our security, our prosperity, and our purpose? Which leader has the vision and the willpower and the backbone? Who will best protect my family?

These are tough questions. And it is the answer to them that has placed me in this hall with you tonight. For the clear answer has left me no choice but to choose country over party. At this defining moment in our history, I stand squarely with you behind the only leaders who can do the job and see it through. George W. Bush and Dick Cheney.

In the speech I gave in this very hall twelve years ago, I quoted FDR and talked about my mama and where I came from. I'd like to continue that story with you tonight.

In the summer of 1940, I was an eight-year-old boy living in a remote little valley in the Appalachian mountains of North Georgia, the son of a widow, a single parent before that term was ever invented. Our country was not yet at war, but adults and children alike knew that some crazy men were across the ocean and they would kill us if they could.

My mama would always have us gather around that old Silvertone radio in our living room to hear what President Roosevelt had to say. In his speech accepting the Democratic nomination that summer, FDR said, "In times like these—in times of great tension, or great crisis—the compass of the world narrows to a single fact." That fact, he said, is the fact of armed aggression aimed at the kind of society we live in. "It is not an ordinary war," he said, "it threatens all men everywhere."

And in that familiar voice, he told us "all private plans, all private lives, have been in a sense *repealed* by an overriding public danger."

In 1940, Wendell Wilkie was the Republican nominee. And there is no better example of someone setting aside "private plans" than this good man. Had Wilkie not been the statesman he was, this country would have entered World War II divided instead of with a common purpose. And the history of the world would have been changed forever. Instead, this Hoosier from Indiana put aside personal ambition to help unite and protect our country against that gathering storm.

This Republican who wanted to be president gave the Democratic incumbent the crucial support needed to institute a peacetime draft, a very unpopular idea at the time. And he made it clear that he would rather lose the election than make it a partisan campaign issue.

At that defining moment in history when a dangerous world needed a united America, that was the Republican challenger's decision. Shortly before he died Wilkie said to a friend, "If I could write my own epitaph and if I had to choose between saying 'Here lies a president' or 'Here lies one who contributed to saving freedom at a moment of great peril,' I would prefer the latter."

Where are such statesmen today? Where is the bipartisanship? Back then, it was said about national security that partisanship stopped at the water's edge. But today, at the same time young Americans are dying in the sands of Iraq and the mountains of Afghanistan, our nation is being torn apart and made weaker because of the Democrats' hatred for George Bush and their manic obsession to prevail politically.

What has happened to the party I've spent my life in? I can remember when most Democrats believed that it was the duty of America to fight for freedom over tyranny.

It was Democratic president Harry Truman who forced a showdown with Stalin and pushed the Red Army out of positions they had occupied in Iran . . .

who came to the aid of the government of Greece when Communist insurgents threatened to overthrow it . . .

who stared down the Soviet blockade of West Berlin by flying in supplies and saving the city from Soviet encroachment.

And in all of this, Republicans supported their Democratic president.

When President Truman was pushing the Marshall Plan to rebuild post-war Germany and France, it was unpopular like the draft had been with FDR in 1940. But once again a Republican, Michigan senator Arthur Vandenburg, chairman of the Senate Foreign Relations, came to the aid of a Democratic administration and, like Wilkie, did what was right for America and the free world.

Time after time in our history, in the face of great danger, Democrats and Republicans have worked together to ensure that freedom would not falter.

But not today. Motivated more by partisan politics than by national security, today's Democratic leaders see America as an occupier, some kind of Darth Vader military empire trying to colonize people.

My father was a World War I veteran who served in France. I never knew him; he died when I was two weeks old. But I can remember wearing his Army coat with sergeant's stripes on it when I was so little it dragged the floor and my arms did not go halfway down its sleeves. Years later I would earn some sergeant stripes myself, in the United States Marine Corps.

And nothing infuriates this Marine more than someone calling American troops occupiers rather than liberators.

Tell that to the one-half of Europe that was freed because Franklin Roosevelt led an army of liberators, not occupiers.

Tell that to the lower half of the Korean Peninsula that is free because Dwight Eisenhower commanded an army of liberators, not occupiers.

Tell that to the half a billion men, women, and children who are free today from the Baltics to the Crimea, from Poland to Siberia, because Ronald Reagan rebuilt a military of liberators, not occupiers.

Now, technically you might label as "occupiers" those U.S. soldiers still in France, but don't expect them to answer. For the only land they are occupying today is found in those thousands of three-by-six-foot gravesites all across Normandy.

There those "occupiers" lie, silent sentinels of sacrifice not for plunder or territory, but for freedom for others.

U.S. soldiers liberate, they don't occupy. Never in the history of the world has any soldier sacrificed more for the freedom and liberty of total strangers than the American soldier.

And, our soldiers don't just give freedom abroad, they preserve it for us here at home.

For it has been said so truthfully that it is the soldier, not the reporter, who has given us the freedom of the press.

It is the soldier, not the poet, who has given us freedom of speech. It is the soldier, not the agitator, who has given us the freedom to protest.

It is the soldier who salutes the flag, serves beneath the flag, whose coffin is draped by the flag who gives that protester the freedom to accuse, abuse, and burn that flag.

No one should dare to even think about being the commander in chief of this country if they don't believe with all their heart, soul, and mind that our soldiers have, are, and always will be liberators abroad and defenders of freedom at home.

But don't waste your breath telling that to the leaders of my party today. In their warped way of thinking, America is the problem, not the solution. America is what's wrong with the world.

They don't believe there is any real danger in the world except that which America brings upon itself through our clumsy and misguided foreign policy. They believe America creates our enemies, be they communists or terrorists.

For every world problem, this crowd always blames America first. They see despotic regimes as nuisances not as threats. Dictators are always given every benefit of the doubt.

They've never seen a threat great enough to require military action. They don't believe that military force has ever solved anything, and that if it did, it shouldn't have.

In their rise to prominence, these head-in-the-sand Democratic leaders have been on the wrong side of history and freedom during the last three decades. It is not their patriotism—it is their judgment that has been so sorely lacking.

They claimed Carter's pacifism would lead to peace. They were wrong.

They claimed Reagan's defense buildup would lead to war. They were wrong.

They claimed militant insurgents across the globe were not communists. Wrong!

They claimed the Strategic Defense Initiative would break our bank, not the back of the Soviet Union. Wrong!

Again and again, time after time, on the major issues that have determined the peace and security of this world, they have been wrong, wrong, wrong!

And no pair has been more wrong, more loudly, more often than the terrible twins of Massachusetts, Ted Kennedy and John Kerry.

Together, Kennedy/Kerry have opposed every single major weapons system that won the Cold War and that are now winning the war on terror.

Listing all the weapon systems that Senator Kerry tried to shut down sounds like an auctioneer selling off our national security, but Americans need to know the facts.

The B-1 Lancer bomber that Senator Kerry opposed dropped 40 percent of the bombs in the first six months of Operation Enduring Freedom in Afghanistan.

The B-2 Spirit that Senator Kerry opposed delivered air strikes against the Taliban in Afghanistan and Hussein's command post in Iraq.

The F-14A Tomcats that Senator Kerry opposed shot down Khaddifi's Libyan MIGs over the Gulf of Sidra.

The modernized F-14D that Senator Kerry opposed delivered missile strikes against Tora Bora.

The F-15 Eagles that Senator Kerry opposed flew cover over our Capitol and New York City after 9/11.

The Apache helicopter that Senator Kerry opposed took out those Republican Guard tanks in Kuwait in the Gulf War.

The Harrier jet that Senator Kerry opposed helped our Marines from Kosovo to Afghanistan, from Bosnia to Iraq.

The Patriot missile Senator Kerry tried to shoot down shot down Saddam's Scud missiles raining down on our soldiers and Israeli citizens during the Gulf War.

I could go on and on and on: *against* the Aegis air-defense cruiser, *against* the Strategic Defense Initiative, *against* the Trident missile . . . against, against, against.

This is the man who wants to be the commander in chief of our U.S. Armed Forces? U.S. forces armed with what? Spitballs?

Twenty years of votes can tell you much more about a man than twenty weeks of campaign rhetoric. Campaign talk tells people who you want them to think you are. Your votes tell people who you really are inside.

Take Kerry's recent posturing on reforming our intelligence system. For years he proposed amendments to slash intelligence funding, even while his more responsible Democratic colleagues were warning him that what he wanted to do would cripple our national security.

Senator Kerry has made it clear that he would use military force only if approved by the United Nations. Guess who that would give a veto to? You've got it. Not exactly someone we would want to trust our loved ones with.

This man, who says he doesn't like outsourcing, wants to outsource our foreign policy to these kinds of folks. That would be the most dangerous outsourcing of all.

This man wants to be leader of the free world. Free for how long?

For more than twenty years, on every one of the great issues of freedom and security, John Kerry has been more wrong, more timid, and more craven than any other national figure. And nothing shows that more clearly than his vote this year to deny funds for our troops in the line of fire and their families back at home.

Like too many of today's Democrats, he believes the one-and-only lesson of history is found in the jungles of Vietnam.

But America's history suggests that's just *one* part of it. The *real* lessons of history lie elsewhere: the waters of Pearl Harbor, the forests of Argonne, the ovens of Auschwitz, the turbulent skies over Germany, and the shores of Normandy.

The *real* lessons of history can be found on the beaches of Iwo Jima, the frozen mountain ridges of Korea, the mass graves of Iraqi deserts, and yes, the halls of the Pentagon, a grassy field in Pennsylvania, and the streets of lower Manhattan not far from here.

George Bush is a commander in chief who understands these real lessons of history. Who understands the price of freedom. Who understands that leaders have to choose between good and evil, tyranny and freedom. And the choice they make will reverberate for generations to come.

President Bush sees the world as it really is, with terrorists who are determined but allies who are timid.

His opponent sees the world as he wishes it were—with terrorists who are timid and allies who are determined. That's not the real world. That's fantasy land, viewed through rose-colored glasses.

George Bush makes it unmistakably plain when he tells terrorists that he will act decisively to defend America. From John Kerry, we get a yes-no-maybe bowl of mush that can only encourage our enemies and confuse our soldiers.

So much for Kerry's foreign policy.

I wish I had time to go into his domestic policy. But I can sum it up in four words: tax, spend, redistribute income. Kerry hopes that if he robs Peter to pay Paul, Paul will vote for him.

I have been in elective office under nine presidents. I've met them all and three I've known very well. George W. Bush is in a class of his own.

I first got to know George Bush when we served as governors together, and I admire and respect this man as I do no other. I am moved by the reverence he shows the first lady and the unabashed love he has for his parents and his daughters.

I identify with this man of faith who has lived that line in "Amazing Grace," "was blind, but now I see." I like the fact that he's the same man on Saturday night as he is on Sunday morning.

I have knocked on the door of this man's soul and found someone home. Someone who can feel the anxiety of an unemployed father in Akron or the suffering of an AIDS victim in faraway Africa.

Someone who is a God-fearing man with a good heart and a spine of tempered steel. A man I would trust with my most precious possession: my family.

This election will forever change the course of history. The only question is how. The answer lies in each of you. Take not the advice of the timid. Step not back but forward.

America's history is living proof that the future belongs not to the fainthearted, but to the brave. Our president is one of the bravest. And that is why tonight when "the compass of the world," as FDR put it, has narrowed to "a single fact," I am honored to join with our president and with you in working to preserve, protect, and defend the United States of America. God bless this great country, and God bless George W. Bush.

INDEX OF NAMES

T

Talmadge, Herman, 55
Taylor, Ray, 217
Thomas, Dylan, 247
Thomas, Evan, 95
Thurmond, Strom, 55
Tillis, Mel, 180
Timberlake, Justin, 198
Toynbee, Arnold, 6
Truman, Harry S., 34-35, 40, 55,
    77, 80, 248, 255
Trump, Donald, 236
Tse-tung, Mao, 149
Turner, Ted, 12, 154
Tyson, Mike, 201, 212

U

Uhler, Lewis K., 135

V

Vandenberg, Arthur, 80, 255
Van Gorder, Charles, 218
Vilsack, Tom, 55

W

Walsh, Ed, 37
Warner, Mark, 104
Washington, George, 171-72, 200
Washington, Peter, 52
Watts, Isaac, 230
Watts, J.C., 47, 65
Wesley, Charles, 185, 230
Weyrich, Paul, 155
Whitman, Christine Todd, 109

Wilkie, Wendell, 40, 80, 254-55
Williams, Hank, 215
Wills, Gary, 101
Wilson, Joe, 95
Wilson, Woodrow, 148
Woodruff, Judy, 88-89, 92, 93
Woodward, Bob, 92

Y

Yeager, Don, 212
Young, Andrew, 50

Z

Zogby, John, 49